OVER 50

and Making a Difference

Be informed. Be influenced. Be inspired.

Diane Priestley

WRITING MATTERS PUBLISHING

OVER 50 and Making a Difference

First published in May 2023 by Writing Matters Publishing

ISBN 978-1-914265-77-8 Pbk

ISBN 978-1-914265-76-1 Ebk

A CIP catalogue record for this book is available from the British Library.

Email dianejoypriestley@gmail.com

Contents

Dedication

Dedicated to Millicent and Garama
and their lovely family,
and all my precious friends in Kenya.
Our vision of making a difference is unfolding.

Introduction

Discover Your Inner Hero

I am a natural campaigner, a passionate activist. Give me a good cause and I will fight for it. This is the essence of who I am.

When I'm campaigning for social justice, human rights, and animal protection, to save the environment, stop wars and prevent all kinds of abuse, I am empowered and fired with confidence, determination and steely focus.

As a child growing up in suburban Melbourne, Australia, I decided to be clever at school. Cleverness was my strategy of choice to win approval and attention. I was the first kid in the classroom to shoot my hand in the air with the correct answer to impress my teacher. I was the eager beaver who did their homework straight away and proudly presented huge project sheets with fancy headings and drawings and diagrams.

Every day after school, I raced home across the park to plonk myself in front of the little black and white telly with a big mug of Milo and handful of biscuits, alongside my cheeky brother, Steve, to watch in riveted awe *The Adventures of Superman.* You know, the original 1950s version starring dashing George Reeves.

But it wasn't the invincible caped flying man who captured my adoration. That feisty female reporter, Lois Lane was my idolised hero.

She was my first 'career woman' role model; a fearless investigative journalist who scooped the front-page story with her by-line! Lois Lane inspired me to become a crusading newspaperwoman.

At the age of 11 in Grade Six, I discovered the school newsletter and the power of the roneo machine to mass produce *my* stories with *my* by-line to go into every home in the district! My first published article was about my cat! I felt 10 feet tall!

While an amusing story about my lazy cat led to my first euphoric taste of being published, my passion for causes erupted when I was 16 in Form Five at high school. The year was 1973. We could choose our own topic to research for our Modern History assignment. I chose the Vietnam War. That's when my eyes were opened to the horrors of war inflicted on innocent men, women and children and their humble homes and communities by foreign governments with the power to kill, maim and destroy. I was outraged and became a budding peace activist.

At 17, in my final year of high school, I was reading late into the night, not my prescribed Literature classics, but disturbing books about the abject cruelty and mass killing of animals for food. I was convinced by the well-reasoned case for going vegetarian and eagerly boycotted this abhorrent social norm by adopting a healthy, meat-free diet. I became a staunch and vocal 'veggie' and harangued everyone at the dinner table about the horrors of abattoirs.

Then in my third year of university in 1978, the inspiring South African Journalist, Donald Woods gave a stirring speech to students about the despicable Apartheid system and the murder of courageous black Activist, Steve Biko by police who beat him to death in custody. I was infuriated by racism, persecution, and subjugation.

The fire in my belly about injustice and inequality burned into my soul. I wrote a passionate double-page article for the student newspaper.

In my Journalism studies, I learned about the 'power of information' to change the world. As an eager cadet newspaper reporter, my role was to gather and disseminate information to the public, writing in strong journalistic style. Reports had to be newsworthy, attention-grabbing, concise, and easy to understand.

Daily news was churned out fast and furious to meet deadlines. The smoky newsroom was crammed with frantic reporters bashing away on noisy typewriters. I grabbed this exciting challenge with both hands and loved my profession in the print media. I had found my Purpose.

Disseminating information combined with my youthful zeal for social justice and human rights infused my writing when I was promoted to Women's Editor with the daily broadsheet, the *Geelong Advertiser*. Throughout my energetic 20s, I championed causes with irrepressible enthusiasm.

In my mature 30s, my husband, Andrew and me and our two kids, Daniel and Justine, moved north to Queensland. After a stint with *Quest Newspapers* in Brisbane, I landed a job with the *Sunshine Coast Daily* in this idyllic, tropical region boasting pristine surf beaches and lush rainforests.

For 10 years, I wrote a heart-warming, humorous weekly column, *Family Matters* about the joys and challenges of family life and a vast array of colourful features on community and environmental issues.

When elected as a Councillor on *Maroochy Shire Council* in the 90s, I relished the chance to support projects to protect koala habitat and the beautiful Buderim Forest, support funding for the fledgling university, and publicise child abuse prevention campaigns.

In my reflective 40s, my career took another turn when I studied counselling and psychology and set up a practice. But I soon discovered I was more interested in writing about psychology than the intensity of one-to-one therapy.

I missed journalism and the fulfilment of reaching a mass readership. When I started writing the informative weekly column, *Relationship Matters* for the Queensland-wide newspaper, the *Courier-Mail*, I was back in my element.

But at 47, I experienced a midlife crisis and entered the 'dark night of the soul' for three years until I emerged a stronger, deeper human being.

In my revitalised 50s, I was struck with the desire to move to the UK to explore life on the other side of the world from our far-flung continent. Our son had already moved to London and was making a splash in business circles. Our daughter was ready to fly the comfortable nest and experience the multicultural melting pot of Earls Court.

When Andrew and I lobbed in West London in 2009, at first, I was thrilled by big city life, soaking up musicals on the West End, and travelling Europe and writing delightful travel stories for *50 Connect*. And I wrote reports on health and global issues for *Mediaplanet*, distributed through the UK Guardian.

But soon another powerful urge surfaced. I wanted a Purpose. I wanted a cause to champion and worthy charities to support. My youthful passion for social justice and human rights stirred in my belly again.

Two more epiphanies in 2011 and 2013 propelled me into pursuing community work in Africa. Along the way I weaved a philosophy about the benefits of mature-aged people over

50 contributing to the world. Read about how my motivation evolved, what I achieved and my exciting vision for the future.

I hope this book inspires you to find the cause that recharges your brain, calls your heart, and ignites a fire in your belly. Maybe you will find your inner hero. Together we can create a fair, equal, peaceful, kind, loving and flourishing planet for all.

In her soul-stirring book, *The Hero Within*, Carol S. Pearson explores six Jungian archetypes: the Innocent, the Orphan, the Wanderer, the Warrior, the Altruist, and the Magician that guide us on the heroic journey of life. In our mature years, the Warrior fights for what's right, the Altruist sacrifices for others and the Magician has the power to transform.

She writes: "When the Magician archetype is activated, you feel confident that you know what ought to be done to transform your life or your world. You stop letting others make your decisions, and you develop a vision for where you want to go. You are willing to risk action – to get behind the wheel of your life. You activate the gear stick of magic when you begin to act in keeping with your values and your life purpose."

PART ONE

An Evolving Philosophy

Chapter 1

Turning 50, the Great Divide

Our flamboyant friend celebrated turning 50 with not one, but two, spectacular parties with hundreds of guests. He even jumped out of a plane, thanks to the surprise skydiving present from his kids!

Turning 50 is a big deal, a major milestone. Of course, all birthdays with a zero on the end are significant as they mark entry into a new decade but somehow 50 represents the 'great divide', a sharp line between young and old has been crossed.

Fifty means you have lived for half a century on the planet, witnessing half a century of world history. Now that is something! You have seen some sights, experienced euphoric highs and anguished lows, learned some stuff and clocked some serious miles on the 'journey of life'.

And somehow you sense with trepidation that you are entering new territory. You are no longer at the beginning of the exciting journey, all innocent, fresh and perky with your packed lunch, just setting out. No, you are somehow weary and jaded and a little vulnerable from life's knocks, facing the homeward trek.

Yes, you have just entered the latter stage of life.

Three-Act Movie

Some optimists, hopeful of living to 100, imagine we are in the 'second half' of life! But unless we live to 100, the age of 50 is not exactly 'midlife'. I prefer the concept of 'three acts of life'. In the three acts of a movie, the drama is divided into the Orientation, Complications and Resolution. Some philosophers view the lifespan as 90 years and divide the nine decades into 'acts' of three decades: Act One is birth through childhood, the teens and the 20s; the Middle Act is the 30s, 40s and 50s and the Final Act of life is the 60s, 70s and 80s plus any bonus years.

In this concept of the lifespan, the 50s is the final decade of the Middle Act of life, with plenty of zest to take on the world, which then sets you up for a meaningful final act.

Acclaimed researcher and writer, Gail Sheehy has another way of viewing the lifespan. In her inspiring book, *New Passages* she explores the idea of 'A Second Adulthood' that starts forming around 45 and dubs the fifties decade 'The Flaming Fifties'. She writes: "As the years go by, your warmth and curiosity, your ease in relating to people, your intelligence and imagination, your wit and sense of irony all become more important than looks to the package of attributes that people appreciate about you."

How does the 50 milestone compare to turning 40? Many people face 40 with dread, believing they have reached the plateau of Life's Mountain, and 'It's all downhill from here'. Humorous birthday cards gloat about your inevitable demise!

But I recall being full of bravado, celebrating this pinnacle in grand style, with the Mayor and honoured guests at a fancy dinner party in a beautiful restaurant.

I saw myself at the peak of my maturity but still youthful, attractive, vibrant, popular and in demand, full of ambition and new projects, still raising kids and racing around in top gear.

My midlife crisis came at 47 as I approached the Big Five-Oh with rising panic. I didn't buy a motorbike or get a tattoo. Instead, I took off to New York to live out a lost fantasy as a carefree single. It ended in tears. I returned to my marriage and picked up the shattered pieces.

Age is Relative

Perception of age is subjective and depends on where you are perched on the lifespan. When we are children, teenagers, or 20-something, it is impossible to imagine ever being 50. It's just too far off in the distance. And anyone over 30 is ancient. When you are young and beautiful, all wrinkly people with grey hair and glasses are seen as 'elderly', one murky blur with no distinctions between 50s, 60s, 70s and 80s; they are just a generic group of geriatrics!

When I was 39, I wrote a heartfelt newspaper column lamenting my age and how everyone in the newsroom was suddenly younger than me. My feisty 82-year-old yoga teacher was indignant and reprimanded me in front of the whole class. "How dare you claim you are old," she barked, while we were all in Downward Dog!

Whatever our age, we will always be younger or older than someone else. The eight-year-old is older than her five-year-old brother. As the profound poem Desiderata advises: 'If you compare yourself with others, you may become vain and bitter.

For always there will be greater and lesser persons than yourself.'

Subjective Age

How old you perceive yourself internally is another matter. Baby Boomers, the generation born during the 18 years following the Second World War, between 1946 and 1964, generally perceive themselves as 15 years younger than their chronological age. My generation, who were teenagers in the radical 60s and 70s have a tough time ageing, clinging desperately to youth, still loading up the van and heading for Glastonbury!

Now what does Desiderata says about clinging to youth? 'Take kindly the counsel of the years, gracefully surrendering the things of youth.' Might be wise to give up partying until 3am and get to bed before midnight!

There's another twist to the concept of 'age'. We all have three ages: chronological age - the number of years you've lived; biological age - the condition of your organs and body systems and your psychological age – how old you feel, think and act! It's possible to exude youthfulness and vitality beyond 50 and way into your senior years.

Renowned Hypnotherapist, Marisa Peer writes in her book, *You Can Be Younger*: "The age you are in years is irrelevant, because we have three ages and three different ways of measuring our age. We have a chronological age, a biological age, and a psychological age.

"Our psychological age is the age we feel, and this can change from moment to moment. Listening to music from the past, dancing, laughing, being childlike rather than childish, and splashing in puddles or giggling all cause us instantly to feel younger. This feeling sends a message to our bodies, which then literally begin to grow younger, making younger hormones and younger chemicals."

Human Biologist, Dr Julia Jones, in her ground-breaking book, *Neuron*, explains that the key to a long, healthy life is aligning daily habits to our natural biological systems. She calls these positive habits 'biohacks'.

On the importance of sleep, she writes: "When our conscious mind is asleep, the brain is still at work, consolidating memories, removing toxins built up during the day and thoroughly restoring the body ready for action tomorrow. Lack of quality sleep over a prolonged period is now shown to be linked with degenerative brain diseases. Sleep is essential to good health."

In the book, *Facing The Fifties*, author, Peter A. O'Connor says it takes a person five years to 55 to admit they are in fact in their 50s! He says it is essential to move from denial to reflection. He believes we face an inner struggle between the forces of Eros (Life) and the forces of Thanatos (Death). Ultimately, we must emerge grabbing life with both hands, with real gusto, not ambivalence.

Become a Wise Elder

Pioneering Psychologist, Erik Erikson, writing from 1950 to 1982, extended the work of Freud and Jung from childhood development into a study of the entire lifespan. He claimed that there are eight stages of life with a psychological task or challenge at each stage.

In Middle Adulthood we must embrace 'Generativity' over Self Absorption. We must learn to care for others, our families and communities and sow good seeds into the next generation.

In Old Age, Erikson says we need to embrace Integrity over Despair and share our wisdom with the world. If we fail to become 'wise elders', we risk shrivelling up, crippled by a sense of failure and despair.

Meantime, in facing the great divide of 50, the blunt fact is you are either getting older or you are dead. Personally, I prefer the first option. I am grateful to still be alive when so many others are less fortunate and have not lived to this age.

To live every day with gratitude for the wondrous gift of life is the only positive attitude to cultivate in response to the inevitability of ageing.

Years ago, I took my daughter for riding lessons on a horse property on the Sunshine Coast hinterland run by a hardy old horse whisperer and his cheerful wife, both active in their 80s.

On arrival at the shed, I'd say: "How are you Frank?" His eyes would twinkle under his battered cowboy hat, his face would erupt in a radiant smile, and he'd hit me with his favourite joke: "I'm fantastic! I woke up this morning and I was still here!"

Old Frank would laugh with glee. And Grace would chuckle, too!

Chapter 2

How My MADness Took Hold

The crunchy golden leaves were falling on a reflective autumn day in October 2011. I was sitting in the stylish Mermaid Theatre near St Paul's Cathedral, in the buzzing audience of an inspirational event organised by my spectacularly successful son, Daniel, who at the tender age of 21 started his own company, *Triumphant Events* in Australia.

And now, less than 10 years later he was gracing the stage in London, a charismatic speaker, leading the 'entrepreneur revolution', motivating Brits to reject the doom and gloom of the recession and fight back by starting their own businesses and living their dreams.

I was incredibly proud of my son but dejected and frustrated about my own life. My promising new job in the UK after we had relocated from Australia had suddenly fallen in a heap. I was forced to start all over again. In that rarefied anything-is-possible atmosphere, I asked myself: 'What do I really want to do with the rest of my life?'

In my mid-50s, I wanted to use my lifetime of experience, knowledge and talents to make a meaningful contribution to the world, not slide aimlessly into early retirement. I wanted to work in poor countries and help alleviate the immensity of human suffering.

But how could I make this heartfelt desire a reality? That catalytic day launched me into a frenzy of brainstorming and research. I hatched the idea to start MAD for humanity, using the catchy acronym for Making A Difference.

If I wanted to make a positive difference, then plenty of other men and women of my generation of feisty 'Baby Boomers' did too. I decided to organise trips for adventurous mature-aged women and men to volunteer with projects in Africa, while also experiencing the magnificent countryside and wildlife. I had stumbled into the brave new frontier of 'voluntourism'.

Over three months, I approached leading charities to enquire if they needed teams of mature-aged volunteers. I wanted to partner with worthy organisations and add value, not so much in monetary donations, but value measured in human skills, expertise, and heart.

I realised I would need to build an impressive website, generate publicity and climb a steep learning curve, mastering countless travel, health and legal details of working in foreign countries. It dawned on me that this massive project would take ages to set up. Such MADness could consume me for the next 10 years! But still I was undaunted.

Blinding Flash of the Obvious

But thank goodness for a BFO! (Blinding Flash of the Obvious) Perhaps I should google 'MAD'? That's when I struck gold! Eureka! In January 2012, I discovered *Madventurer*, a vibrant website about an amazing voluntourism organisation for energetic young students on their gap year.

Now this was an intersection of dreams!

Madventurer is a well-established social enterprise, having grown and thrived since 1998, the brainchild of a remarkable, visionary Engineering Graduate John Lawler, inspired by his own life-changing gap year in a village in Ghana.

For 25 years, teams of young volunteers have helped build and renovate schools, pre-schools, orphanages, clinics and water and sanitation systems in poor communities around the world.

Another BFO! Why re-invent the wheel? Why not partner with *Madventurer*, adding a new dimension, a niche market of MAD older men and women?

While some mature-aged volunteers might not be keen on heavy construction work, they could offer their knowledge and skills in fields such as medical, counselling, education, micro business, crafts, farming and food, mentoring adults and nurturing children.

Volunteering is a two-way street; improving quality of life for people unfairly disadvantaged by poverty while enriching well-off volunteers, whose materialistic lives can ironically feel empty, with a revived sense of purpose and paradigm shift of values.

Volunteering heals the denial and disconnection between affluent and poor countries so that cultures can join hands and people of all colours can form heart to heart bonds of friendship with mutual respect and equality.

By pitching in, volunteers help correct the unjust imbalance between those who live in excessive consumption and those who live in abject deprivation. Yes, ordinary people, despite destructive politics, can change the world.

In the depth of winter in 2012, I threw on my coat and scarf and travelled up north by train to Newcastle-upon-Tyne to meet with John and discuss how we might collaborate! To my absolute delight he embraced the idea of expanding Madventurer to cater for mature-aged volunteers and welcomed me on the next trip. My dream of volunteering in Africa was about to come true.

Volunteering In Ghana

In the summer of 2012, while London was excited about the Queen's Diamond Jubilee and the Olympic Games, I headed to Ghana on the west coast of Africa to volunteer with *Madventurer* and experience poverty up close and personal.

That life-changing experience led to the publication of my book, *Adventurers in Ghana* and a hunger for humanitarian work that would never be satisfied by little nibbles. Ten years later my appetite has grown and I'm eager for more!

I am inspired by the brilliant TV series, *Wild At Heart*. The lead character, played by the talented Stephen Tompkinson, is a vet in Bristol who earns a good living treating pet cats and dogs. Circumstances thrust him into a new life in the wilds of South Africa where he rescues, performs operations, and saves endangered species.

The same ordinary skillset becomes extraordinary in a different setting where the need for his veterinary skills is immense. His work becomes life-changing and planet-saving. His dull life is transformed, and he finds meaning and purpose.

The transformation from ordinary to extraordinary is possible for all of us when we use our skills where they are needed most. We can Make a Difference to humanity, wild animals and the planet.

Chapter 3

My MAD Manifesto

Not so much crazy, but I'm *mad* in the sense of *angry* about the suffering, injustice and inequality in the world. That's why the acronym MAD for Making A Difference is the perfect call to action.

Mature men and women have much to contribute to the world. With our kids grown up, empty nesters often yearn for a new lease on life. We look beyond our homes and families to unknown frontiers, with a renewed sense of adventure.

Having raised children, overcome a multitude of challenges, and often survived heartbreak, we are wounded warriors, equipped with natural nurturing abilities and empathy and compassion.

We have an abundance of intelligence and wisdom, career and life experience, talents and skills to offer the world. We have a sense of urgency and eagerness not to waste our gifts; a burning desire to contribute to humanity, protect the natural environment and give generously of ourselves.

But ironically just when we have the most to offer with undivided time and focus, devotion and passion, we are often considered unemployable and consigned to the scrapheap of invisible retirement.

Many of us capable, multi-skilled women who juggled exhaustive roles as supportive wives, caring mothers and devoted workers find ourselves when we're over 50 cast aside as unwanted, useless, and redundant in the workforce. And mature-aged men often experience obsolescence in the Millennial techie workplace.

American Obstetrician and Gynaecologist, Christiane Northrup, writes, in her book, *The Wisdom of Menopause*: "Throughout most of human history, the vast majority of women died before menopause; for those who survived, menopause was experienced as a signpost of imminent and inevitable physical decline.

"But today, with a woman's life expectancy averaging between 78 and 84, it is reasonable to expect that she will not only live 30 to 40 years beyond menopause, but be vibrant, sharp, and influential as well. The menopause you will experience is not your mother's (or grandmother's) menopause."

You're Hired!

We must employ ourselves and find our own causes to champion in a world of hardship and suffering crying out for help. We must hire ourselves to take on this real work that gives meaning and purpose and deep fulfilment.

We must not depend on the establishment to recognise our value. We must recognise our value, even if others don't! Over 50 we must seize the challenge of venturing into new territory. Grasp the nettle even though it hurts!

Baby Boomers (the generation born post-World War 2, 1946-64) are old enough and wise enough to be our own parent and employer; to rely on our own inner guidance, trust our own discerning judgement and make our own decisions.

When we discover and affirm our worth and begin to live by our core values, we will realise we can generate income, solve problems, and add value to the world. Empowered mature-aged men and women can inform, influence, and inspire through their words, feelings and actions and enrich, heal, and transform lives.

However, don't go solo. We must not attempt tackling social problems alone because isolation is a recipe for failure. Join forces with other dynamic idealists and work together as a united front. We need to overcome rivalry and competitiveness to collaborate in mutual support and co-operation. Together people over 50 can Make a Difference for humanity and the planet.

Ubuntu is an ancient African word meaning 'I am what I am because of who we all are'.

The late Archbishop of Cape Town, Desmond Tutu wrote in his book, *No Future Without Forgiveness*: "Ubuntu is the essence of being human. Ubuntu speaks about the fact that you can't exist as a human being in isolation. It speaks about our interconnectedness. You can't be human all by yourself. And when you have this quality of ubuntu you are known for your generosity.

We think of ourselves far too frequently as just individuals, separated from one another, whereas we are connected. What you do affects the whole world. When you do well, it spreads out for the whole of humanity.

A person with ubuntu is generous, hospitable, friendly, caring and compassionate. They share what they have.

It also means my humanity is caught up, is inextricably bound up, in yours. We belong in a bundle of life.

A person is a person through other people. Ubuntu means *I am human because I belong.*"

Chapter 4

Finding Purpose in Later Life

Rather than older people focusing on what the world can do for them, I want you to consider what you can do for the world! We have a lifetime of wisdom, caring and skills to share. And altruistic work brings deep fulfilment. Giving to others brings a sense of purpose, passion and empowerment in later life.

Older people should go MAD in a good way! This desire to Make a Difference usually takes a firm hold when we hit 50. We yearn to make a positive contribution to our families, our local community, our country or global issues. We are bursting with a lifetime of accumulated knowledge and wisdom, empathy and caring, skills and talents. And we want to enrich younger generations with all we have to offer. When our kids grow up and become independent adults, it's possible to embrace a whole new lease on life. We have the freedom to reinvent ourselves!

However, one of the problems older people can face is becoming too 'self-centred' and fixated on their ailments and grievances. I understand that many people are dealing with chronic pain and serious illnesses that require focus on self-care.

For healthy women and men over 50, the solution is to become 'other-centred'. We all need to ask ourselves: 'How can I improve the world by alleviating suffering and increasing joy? How can I prevent abuse and exploitation and cultivate caring and human rights? How can I overcome inequality and deprivation and promote fairness and prosperity for all? How can I help to stop environmental destruction and protect animals and our precious planet?'

Ironically, resisting self-absorption and shifting to an outward focus benefits our own health and wellbeing. There are rich rewards in being altruistic. Devotion to others brings a sense of purpose, deep fulfilment and empowerment. Or to indulge in a snappy alliteration: purpose, passion and power!

The opposite state of mind as we age is a miserable option: a bleak sense of futility, emptiness and helplessness, while wallowing in self-pity and resentment, blaming the new fast-paced, high-tech workplace for throwing us on the scrapheap, stamped 'obsolete'.

The Need to be Needed

All human beings have basic emotional needs to be loved, needed, wanted, respected, appreciated and valued. These needs don't stop at 50! Mature-aged people must play a valuable role in the community as wise elders, earning respect and appreciation from the young. Sadly, in our youth-worshiping culture, us older people are often not respected for our decades of life experience, our deep well of knowledge and the unique skills and talents we've mastered.

Rather than complaining and blaming young people for their bad attitude, it's up to us to be pro-active and create a valuable role for ourselves within our families as helpful grandparents, in our local neighbourhoods, in national organisations or venture to other countries to support those in dire need of our expertise.

Canadian Counsellor, Steve Rose, PhD, writes: "The need to be needed is an individual's sense of significance rooted in the sense of being part of a community or cause beyond themselves.

The need to be needed is one of our fundamental desires. We want to feel significant in the eyes of others, even if it is only one other person. We want to feel like we play an important role, whether in an organization, family, or life of another.

The need to be needed is rooted in our need for a sense of contribution to something beyond ourselves."

Decades of Searching

Let me tell you a little more of my story. We were happy living on the Sunshine Coast in Australia. With a carefree beach lifestyle, an ideal place for raising our kids, my husband and I had successful, thriving careers. I enjoyed a high profile as a newspaper journalist and popular columnist and local government councillor and in my 40s studied psychology and became a counsellor.

And then in 2009 we were ready for a major life change and fresh challenges. I had wanted to live in the UK since my 20s. Like many ambitious young Aussie journalists, I aspired to a trailblazing career on Fleet Street in those glory days of the 1970s and 80s. Growing up in Australia, I felt displaced and isolated from the rest of the world, with my appetite for travelling and exploring and global issues.

So, we moved to London, which was thrilling! I devoured a cultural feast of musical shows and concerts, weekend jaunts exploring the genteel English countryside, historic castles and quaint villages and was blessed with a lifelong dream of being a travel writer, with enviable trips to picturesque destinations in Europe.

Moving to the UK was a homecoming for me, returning from the far-flung colony where my English, Irish and Scottish ancestors, some convicts, had been transported and incarcerated for petty crimes. Other grandparents were courageous sole migrants who left their distraught families for the unknown, untamed continent 10,000 miles across the oceans.

But this Aussie returned to her ancestral homeland to embrace bustling, multicultural West London and then the tranquillity of rural Kent, where we lived with our cocker spaniels and hens, revelling in the changing seasons.

For a few years I didn't miss being hot and sweaty in the sweltering tropics. Cosy in my coat and boots, I delighted in crisp walks in the woodlands and cheerful daffodils and shimmering carpet of bluebells come spring!

You would think this pleasant, comfortable life would have been enough for me. But I started to get this gnawing feeling, this MAD desire. Witnessing all the problems of the world, the suffering, poverty, deprivation, trauma and abuse, the horror of war, my heart ached with pain. The extent of tragedy on our planet is overwhelming.

I knew I couldn't solve ALL the problems of the world, so I decided to pick one issue I felt strongly about. This is what I recommend to you: Find your passion and as Henry Thoreau, the great American philosopher, wrote in the 1800s,

"Go confidently in the direction of your dreams!

Live the life you've imagined."

Chapter 5

The Art of 'Generativity'

Almost every year since moving to the UK in 2009, I would return to Australia to stay with my mum in the retirement village. The residents had lovely little homes with pretty gardens, a swimming pool and community halls set on shady parkland with a tranquil lake teeming with chirpy birds. Compared to the poor communities I'd visited; this was a high standard of living.

Some of the elderly residents had twinkling eyes, hearty laughter and full calendars! Like the irrepressible Joy and Jeff, in their 90s, who rode their bicycles everywhere, volunteered in their church and saw the good in everyone!

Other residents were full of bitterness and petty grievances. One old man was convinced his gardening spade had been stolen, an indignant old lady was furious about the bossy bitch who has taken over the social committee.

In loud conversations on driveways, they compared and competed about their painful ailments, the heart scares, the bad knees, the hip ops, the emergency hospital visits, without listening or caring about the other's suffering.

Another faction vilified, in vicious huddles, those horrible dogs that left messes on their manicured lawns and vehemently condemned irresponsible dog-owners. 'They should be thrown in jail!' they shouted.

The wrinkled, hunched old wives would grip the flabby arms of their senile husbands when a younger woman walked by and smiled 'Hello'; jealously guarding the old relic and oozing envy and grief for her lost youth, buried with photo memories deep in the drawer with the sparkly earrings she once wore, dazzling the dance floor with haughty elegance!

I am fearful of ending up like this; shrinking smaller and smaller and withering, bitter and twisted, lonely and isolated, in a segregated old people's village, discarded by mainstream community, waiting…waiting for something? What is it? Are these cranky old folks aching for Grace; for Love to swoop in, like a huge soft white dove, and cradle them, a visit from the ungrateful grown-up children who are busy with their interesting lives.

Perhaps they are waiting for genuine friendship that pierces their dense armour of complaints and touches the heart with lightness, joy, humour, and gratitude for still being alive! Or perhaps they are waiting to be recognised as useful, the realisation by youngsters that all their years of experience must be good for something!

Erikson's Theory of Human Development throughout our Lifespan

Erik Erikson was a German-born American developmental psychologist and psychoanalyst (1902 – 1994) who extended the developmental theories of Sigmund Freud to include the entire lifespan.

Erikson identified eight stages of development, not just in childhood, but also right throughout life into old age and death. He claimed each stage held an inherent struggle and desired outcome.

Erikson's eight stages comprise:

- Stage One: Birth to age one, the baby has to resolve a crisis between Trust and Mistrust of parents or caregivers with the desired outcome of Hope.
- Stage Two: from one to two, the toddler grapples with Autonomy versus Shame and Doubt with the desired outcome of Will.
- Stage Three: from age three to five, the young child faces a crisis of Initiative over Guilt within the family with the desired outcome of Purpose.
- Stage Four: From age six to 11, the child is challenged with Industriousness over Inferiority at school with a desired outcome of Competence.
- Stage Five: Adolescence, brings conflict between Identity and Role Confusion within peer groups with the desired outcome of Fidelity, the ability to be true to an integrated sense of self.
- Stage Six: Young Adulthood, the challenge is finding Intimacy over Isolation with a spouse and amongst friends with the desired outcome of Love.
- Stage Seven: Middle Adulthood is where we are challenged to discover 'generativity', a term coined by Erikson, rather than self-absorption. This requires us to contribute to our family, community and work. The desired outcome is Care.
- Stage Eight: In Old Age, the final stage of life, we face a struggle between Integrity and Despair. And the desired outcome is Wisdom.

Generativity means the ability to look beyond yourself and to express concern for the future of the world and younger generations. In contrast, the self-absorbed person is preoccupied with personal wellbeing and material gain.

It is no wonder that, like many others, when I turned 50, I was hit with an overpowering desire to Make a Difference to the world. I wanted to contribute to solving problems and reducing suffering on a global level. Having lived more than half of my life, the balance was tipped to the approach of the end, and I started thinking about legacy, concerned about what I would leave behind after I'm gone.

So that is when my husband and I migrated from Australia to the UK to be close to the centre of the world stage, where we felt better placed to make a positive difference to global issues.

In 2012, I volunteered in Ghana and published my book in April 2013 and hosted a Book Launch with my proud mum and close friends in Australia. That amazing year I was lucky to take exciting press trips to Switzerland and Spain and delightful family trips to France and Italy. We had moved to the countryside, and finally I had my gorgeous cocker spaniel puppy, Honey. I was content but still not satisfied that I was achieving enough.

Soul Searching to Uncover My Talents

On my 57th birthday in December 2013, Andrew and I had a night out in London and saw the brilliant stage show, *War Horse*, with incredibly talented, creative performers operating intricate life-like puppets, singing, dancing and acting with utter perfection to tell a glorious, triumphant story.

Just as attending my son's inspiring event in 2011 had sparked my MAD desire, seeing the magnificent *War Horse* stirred another epiphany.

The next day, I took to my bed with my journal and tried to figure out what I was good at! I realised that I am not a perfectionist who could spend hours every day for years mastering an instrument or difficult skill like those talented performers in *War Horse*.

I searched my formative years and remembered how I discovered the joy of writing stories at age 11 and the thrill of being published in the school newsletter!

Then at 17, I discovered the empowerment of becoming a vocal campaigner! And I recalled how I was a passionate activist in my 20s; how in my 30s I was elected a local government councillor to work for my community.

In my late 40s I experienced a crisis and wallowed in a bottomless lake of therapy and self-analysis and had to wade my way back to focusing on others. And so, we left the endless summer of coastal Queensland and came to bustling London for a new lease on life. And the years of my fifties had been wonderful, full of city pleasures, travel and adventures!

So at 57, I was reminded of my true Purpose, beyond all the fun, and decided to devote the rest of my life to using my writing skills to campaign for good causes; human rights, peace, animal and environmental protection; all the good stuff that will allow our damaged world to heal, survive and flourish in the future.

I felt that I was finally ready.

I became passionately committed to future generations across Africa discovering their human rights and becoming empowered, free from abuse, suffering and poverty. I claimed my mission for my late fifties and the next decades of my life.

Shifting Focus

If a person in their 50s, 60s and 70s shifts focus to making a difference for others, then he or she will face old age with a sense of dignity, satisfaction and personal fulfillment.

Middle-aged and older people thrive when they use their lifetime of experience to mentor teenagers and young adults or lavish patient love on grandchildren or volunteer in community, environmental or humanitarian projects.

Those mature-aged people who choose to contribute rather than expecting to be coddled by the young are ironically the ones who thrive with a sense of purpose, joy and gratitude, despite their aches and pains.

Elderly people do not have to end up bitter and twisted, nursing grudges and resentment, burdened by a sense of futility and despair, disappointment and failure.

I hope that integrity will defeat despair in your mature years, and you achieve wisdom. Your choice to make a difference is the hope for future generations.

As older people, we need inspiring role models. There is no greater role model than Sir David Attenborough, Broadcaster, Biologist and Natural Historian, who has devoted his life to educating the public about the wonders of wild animals and the magnificence of the natural world in his outstanding BBC documentaries.

Sir David has continued his prolific filmmaking in his 60s, 70s, 80s, and 90s. His stunning work gets better with every breathtaking documentary. In his book, *A Life On Our Planet*, he writes:

"We have come as far as we have because we are the cleverest creatures to have ever lived on Earth. But if we are to continue to exist, we will require more than intelligence. We will require wisdom."

Chapter 6

Rebalancing Our Lop-sided World

We live in a lop-sided world. In one part of the world, we have an over-supply of food, clothing, consumer goods, leisure activities and professional services. While the other part of the world faces an under-supply – a desperate lack – of basic goods and services.

People in rich countries suffer and die from obesity, diabetes, cancer, heart disease and numerous other illnesses due to over-eating unhealthy foods and other harmful habits. While million in poor countries suffer and die from malnutrition, starvation and poverty-related preventable diseases. Extreme excess is juxtaposed with extreme deprivation in a bizarre and tragic global imbalance.

In many poor countries luxurious resorts for the wealthy are just around the corner from villages where local people survive on a few dollars a day. The contrast is shameful.

Inequality between the rich and poor is growing rapidly. The gap between the wealthy elite and the rest of us is widening. The Super Rich, the richest one per cent, have bagged nearly twice as much wealth as the rest of the world put together in the past two years, according to a report by the charity, Oxfam released in January 2023.

The Oxfam *Survival of the Richest* report says: "Billionaire fortunes increase by $2.7 billion (USD) a day. The richest one percent grabbed new wealth worth $23 trillion since 2020. Extreme wealth and extreme poverty have increased simultaneously for the first time in 25 years. Just two years in, this decade is shaping up to be the best yet for billionaires – a roaring 20s boom for the world's richest."

How much wealth does an individual or family *need*? This excessive wealth of the one per cent is sickening and sinister and criminally unjust. This rapaciousness comes at the expense of humanity suffering in poverty.

Meanwhile, we ordinary middle-class folks in the UK, Europe, US, Canada and Australia are spoilt for choice. We are 'lucky' to be able to buy a vast assortment of cheap household and personal goods. We can have anything we want; big screen TVs, hi tech vacuum cleaners, double-door fridges, therapeutic mattresses, comfy furniture, luxury cars, the latest fashion, fancy footwear, exclusive cosmetics, ...you name it, we can have it all...by next day delivery.

We can have all these sparkly consumer goods not because of 'luck' but because they're manufactured in poor countries using low-paid, exploited labour. By 'labour' I mean real flesh and blood, living, breathing, feeling human beings (adults and children) who work gruelling hours hunched over machines or digging in dangerous mines. In the Congo, 20,000 impoverished Congolese people including children dig for toxic cobalt, an ingredient in lithium batteries used in smart phones and electric cars.

We revel in an embarrassment of riches when it comes to entertainment, exotic holidays, and leisure pursuits to fill up our time while people in poor countries struggle just to survive each day without the necessities.

People living in Africa, Asia, Central and South America and the 'under classes' of so called 'rich countries' like the UK and the US struggle for survival every day.

I volunteered with *Shelter*, the charity that supports the Homeless in London, one freezing Christmas to help serve hot meals and try to understand how people end up on the streets. I spoke to men, women and couples who slept on the streets or went to a different hostel every night queuing for a bed. These shattered people had been successful and fallen on hard times; they lost their job, their marriage broke up or they got sick and couldn't cope anymore.

As Crisis workers explained, it is easy for anyone to lose one or more of the pillars of security – income, health and relationships – and fall into homelessness, living rough on the streets and becoming vulnerable to drug and alcohol addiction, prostitution, violence and abuse. These are the hidden social problems of affluent countries.

And globally, wars in Iraq, Afghanistan, Syria, Yemen and other war-torn countries have killed and have maimed millions of innocent men, women and children and destroyed homes and communities and displaced millions around the world who seek safety as refugees. All this destruction is perpetrated by governments, committing crimes against humanity.

Comparing Problems

Compare your First World problems with Third World problems. You can't fit into your jeans after over-indulging in chocolates, cake and wine or burgers and beer! You and your children eat one daily meal of bland maize porridge.

You miss your train by one minute! Damn! Your little daughter walks 10 miles twice a day to a stagnant creek to fetch dirty water for the family to drink.

Having missed your train you get home too late to watch your favourite TV show! Your children don't have shoes, so their feet become infected with diseases and parasites. You are overcharged on your mobile phone usage! Every day you face the indignity of defecating behind a bush because your community doesn't have toilets.

Whenever we face such annoying inconveniences, we can get our problems into perspective by contemplating the horrendous problems of people living in poverty.

Some well-off people are motivated to take action to redress global unfairness. We need to correct the imbalance, so the two extremes find some middle ground.

Older People Can Solve Problems

In our rich, developed world, especially here in London, we also have an over-supply of talented, educated, skilful professionals to compete for the top jobs or the fierce ambition to start their own businesses in an incredibly competitive marketplace.

We have a surplus of women and men aged over 50 with a lifetime of skills, knowledge and wisdom accumulated from successful careers, managing complex lives and raising families. And yet many older people are not wanted in the fast-paced, tech-obsessed, youth-focused workplace.

Sadly, we are mostly redundant, obsolete, superfluous, and consigned to the scrapheap! We are not supposed to say that out loud because fair-minded employers, non-ageist youngsters and feisty oldies will deny this predicament and cite exceptions.

But this lop-sided world is full of irony and unlikely opportunities if you can think outside the box.

Yes, us oldies are in hot demand in poor countries where our skills, knowledge and wisdom plus our heartfelt qualities of nurturing, understanding, kindness, empathy and compassion are welcomed with open arms.

What do we want after we have raised kids to adulthood and given the best of our lives to our chosen vocation? Not just holidays and hobbies, people over 50 have a deep craving to be needed and wanted, respected and valued. We have loads of wisdom and affection to give. We long to share the treasures in our hearts and minds. And the good news is, we can.

Venture Capitalist, pioneering Philanthropist and Author, Sir Ronald Cohen writes in his radical book, *Impact:* "Today the gap between rich and poor has widened massively. Inequality is causing huge migration from poorer countries, especially in Africa, to richer countries in Europe, with people risking their lives to cross the sea in flimsy rubber boats in search of better lives… We need a new system…

This new system is *impact capitalism.*

Impact is an idea whose time has come. Let us move beyond the selfish capitalism of today, overthrowing the dictatorship of profit…Ending the plight of billions and the decline of our planet depends on urgent action. There is a will. There is a way. And there has never been a greater need or better time than right now."

Chapter 7

Soggy Feet, the Queen, the Basics

In the summer of 2016, Save the Children invited me to attend a special event in recognition of my contribution as a volunteer. To be honest, I didn't feel this honour was deserved as I'd only been volunteering for the charity for a year. I was sure there were more worthy people who would leap at the chance to see the Queen. And I felt fraudulent because I was not a royalist, quite the opposite. But the young Volunteer Coordinator insisted.

I recall walking for miles, in heels, from Victoria Station to St James's Park for Her Majesty, the Queen's 90th birthday Patrons' Lunch.

It was pouring with rain and my good suede shoes were saturated and ruined and rubbing a blister into my tender flesh. I had a nasty head cold and my right ear was blocked making me partially deaf. I felt miserable, on the brink of tears. How could such a prestigious event be spoiled by something as natural as rain?

It got me thinking that humans everywhere are simple really when all pretensions are stripped away. All we want is to stay warm and dry when it's wet and cold and cool and shaded when it's scorching hot; to be well and not sick; to have enough food when hungry and enough water when thirsty; to be able to pee and poo in a proper toilet when we need to go; to have comfortable shoes and clothes to protect our bodies and a shelter to call home and feel safe.

Yes these are our basic survival needs and when they are not met, nothing else seems to matter! Not pomp and pageantry. Not even meeting the Queen!

With every painful, soggy step I took, gripping my colourful umbrella against the deluge, I was reminded of my life's mission to ensure that these basic needs are met in far-flung communities where they are denied; where abject poverty and deprivation cheat children and adults of basics survival needs. Many cannot even imagine the luxuries of education, culture and entertainment.

The event for 10,000 guests representing over 600 charities was a spectacular success in the end. I ate my gourmet sandwiches from my beautiful Marks & Spencer picnic hamper, chatting with the other Save the Children volunteers, honoured to be part of this historic event.

We had a view of magnificent Buckingham Palace (comprising 775 lavish rooms) and the golden Victoria Memorial, squashed in the crowd of beaming, loyal royalists draped in plastic ponchos. The sun broke through and the joyful parade paid tribute to legions of volunteers who had devoted decades to serving others, showing the best of humanitarian commitment to alleviating the suffering of fellow human beings.

And by the way, I got to see the Queen! She was wearing hot pink, like me! We humans are not really that different. I bet our Lizzy enjoyed a cup of tea with her feet up, patting her adored corgis, after the pomp and pageantry of her 90th birthday celebrations. The Basics, that's all we need.

As I dared to mention, I am not a royalist. I do not revere the monarchy. I believe that all human beings are of equal value.

I do not believe that wealth should be monopolised by a tiny percentage of the population while the majority struggle. The resources of the world should be shared fairly.

Throughout history colonialism has plundered and exploited Africa and other countries for their rich resources leaving people impoverished and disadvantaged while the wealthy drip with blood diamonds.

The elaborate Coronation of Prince Charles to the position of King Charles in May 2023 is estimated to have cost £250 million in public money. In the same year, the Conservative Government cut social care by £250 million.

British historian, Dr David Olusoga says Kings Charles should pay compensation for the Royal Family's involvement in the slave trade as an act of 'restorative justice' and acknowledge the monarchy's role in the crimes of the Empire.

In my opinion, the British monarchy is an anachronism, at the pinnacle of an oppressive class system that supports unscrupulous governments.

The left and right wings of politics are now irrelevant. A dictatorship is a dictatorship whether you label it communism or fascism. Since 2020 we have seen a global movement by governments to crush human rights. Alternative communities are forming based on equality, fairness, peace, and prosperity for all. This is the hope of the future for We, the People.

Accepting the Nobel Peace Prize in 1964, the great Civil Rights Leader, Martin Luther King said: *"I have the audacity to believe that peoples everywhere can have three meals a day for their bodies, education and culture for their minds, and dignity, equality, and freedom for their spirits."*

Chapter 8

Why Should I Do Humanitarian Work?

When I was 47, I went through a crisis. People joke about midlife crisis but it's no joke when you are wading through misery.

Some people experience a crisis around finances. They lose their job or their business goes bust. Many experience a life-threatening health crisis. Or for others the trauma revolves around relationships. The character flaws, mistakes and unresolved, buried issues of your life reach a volcanic head and erupt spewing forth a flood of pain that engulfs you and your loved ones. A crisis can be an opportunity for healing or the catalyst for a tragic unravelling.

I left my husband and family and ran away to New York. Ostensibly I was looking for career opportunities beyond my coastal hometown in Australia. However, there were unconscious, destructive forces at play, which I later uncovered in therapy. But at the time I boarded that plane I was running on automatic, in a childlike fantasy state.

My escapade ended in tears. I was heartbroken. My heart was shattered into tiny pieces, as if smashed with a sledgehammer. My identity was devastated. I felt completely isolated and alienated; cut adrift, floating in space, ostracised from all ties of love, belonging and security.

I will always remember the precise point of being broken. Consumed by emotional pain, I dropped to my knees while walking in a frenzy, to ease the gut-gnawing anxiety, wrapped in a winter coat, around the frozen lake in Central Park.

And then something happened, in this state of vulnerable humility, my defences in ruins, my eyes streaming with tears. I was overwhelmed with empathy. Suddenly, I felt empathy for my husband and children. I felt the pain I'd caused them, through my mistakes and failures. I saw my selfish actions from their perspective. I recalled everyone I had hurt and damaged throughout my life. The pain was overwhelming. But this was pain for others, not self-pity.

A Spiritual Awakening

This is when I experienced remorse; a kind of living death; grief and sorrow for everyone I'd ever hurt. I'd arrived at the moment of truth, kneeling before my Maker.

Something else happened; a spiritual awakening. I knew in my broken heart that I needed a saviour. I cried out to God to forgive my sins. I'd heard about this kind of confession and praying for forgiveness in Sunday School, but it was just a story then. This experience was real.

I found my way to a Baptist Church in Harlem and collapsed into the loving arms of my black soul sisters and brothers, conspicuously the only white person in the congregation. After a few weeks of sobbing through hymns, I answered the alter call and accepted Christ as my saviour and guiding light and I was baptised in that beautiful, comforting church before hopping on the plane at JFK and heading home to save my marriage and family.

I started my walk of Repentance; an intensive process of soul searching. I attended church and workshops, read copious psychology and theology books, journalled, did counselling sessions and group therapy and delved deep into my psyche, my childhood and my entire past. I regressed, regretted, reproached myself, grieved, cried, made connections, gained insights, and emerged a wiser woman. This I believe is called the Ashes stage of life.

Healing Old Wounds

I came to understand myself and heal old wounds. I learned positive new core values to replace distorted beliefs formed from early traumas. I developed new qualities of forgiveness, grace, devotion, gratitude, joy, kindness, understanding, empathy and compassion.

That harrowing introspective passage, the Dark Night of the Soul, lasted three years from 2004. It was 2007, when I turned 50, that I began to feel normal again, strong and whole inside and enriched with deeper qualities of a mended heart.

Through this process of Repentance, which means to 're-think' your whole life, I was rewarded with the seven R's: Resurrection, Redemption, Renewal, Restoration, Reclamation, Reconciliation and Recovery.

We did rebuild our marriage and close, loving family on a new foundation of solid values and in 2009 moved countries to pursue shared dreams of expanded horizons.

When I sat at my desk in our tranquil home in rural England, perched on the edge of a new year, the Year 2016, I realise I emerged from that painful cocoon nine long years ago. I had clocked up almost a whole decade of living, travelling and writing since then.

If Repentance is an inner process of reviewing and transforming your emotional and mental state, there must be something beyond the wallowing that imbues this agonising process with a higher purpose.

New Life

I've come to believe that on the other side of the soul-searching journey is a wide-open, glorious vista of New Life. While Repentance focuses on Thinking and Feeling, the exciting stage of New Life focuses on Doing. At last, it's time to put into action those endless hours of introspection.

Christianity calls this next stage of the journey Atonement, where we get to make amends for the mistakes and sins of our life; to do good instead of harm. I have arrived at a place of courage and empowerment with a desire to help those in need. This genuine desire goes beyond childish self-centredness to mature altruism.

I'm fascinated by two scriptures, which are blatant calls to action. In Matthew 25, Jesus tells his disciples:

"I was hungry and you fed me,

I was thirsty and you gave me a drink,

I was homeless and you gave me a room,

I was shivering and you gave me clothes,

I was sick and you stopped to visit,

I was in prison and you came to me.

Then those sheep are going to say, 'Master what are you talking about? When did we ever see you hungry and feed you, thirsty and give you a drink? And when did we ever see you sick or in prison and come to you?"

Then the King will say, 'I'm telling you the truth: Whenever you did one of these things for someone overlooked or ignored, that was me – you did it to me."

Practical Christianity

Since reading this scripture years ago, I've had a smouldering desire to join with like-minded people in devoting myself to humanitarian work to feed the hungry, give water to those deprived of this basic need, provide education for children and jobs for men and women, medical centres for communities and freedom from the imprisonment of abject poverty.

The time arrived in 2016 to start my work in Africa. It took all those years but that's okay. There is a perfect season for everything in the unforced rhythms of grace.

> And Jesus gives a parable about investment. A man goes on a trip and gives his three servants a sum of money each to invest while he's away. He gives one $5000, the second $2000 and the third $1000. The first and second servant went ahead and doubled their money and the master was pleased with their efforts when he returned. But the third servant hid his money in a safe place and refunded the exact amount to his master who was furious that he wasted the opportunity.

I don't think this lesson is about investing money; it's about investing your God-given talents to do the most good. I don't want to get to the end of my life with my little bundle of talents wrapped up nice and neat under a bush! I want to invest my talents to get the best Return on Investment!

I believe we reach a mature stage of life where we have an accumulation of experience, talents, skills, abilities and qualities to use in the best way possible for the benefit of others.

Assess Your Talents

I have modest talents. I can research and understand issues and disseminate information through writing in the media. I can inform, influence and inspire.

I have qualifications and skills in psychology and can offer counselling and workshops to educate and empower girls and women, boys and men, about human rights.

I know about plant-based nutrition and can cook healthy food and nurture, love and support subsistence communities in Africa.

From leading committees on Council, to project managing building houses and organising travel itineraries, I'm an organiser and can manage all kinds of projects.

My accumulated skillset isn't extraordinary however if I invest it wisely I can give the world maximum value. At nearly 60, although I had enjoyed a colourful career, I felt I had not achieved my potential. I had so much more to give. Some heroic people achieve their potential early and lead full lives and die young. Others like me need a whole lifetime to reach our potential!

Everyone's altruistic calling is different. We must all find the cause that fits our skillset and personality. Some grandparents devote their mature years to their families and local communities. Others have a global vision.

Over 50 we often go in search of the Lost Self of our youth. I know mature-aged people who actively track down and re-connect with teenage sweethearts in pursuit of the thrilling vitality of those heady days.

Finding My Teenage Activist

However, I want to reclaim the passionate campaigner of my youth. I want to re-activate the fiery, outspoken young girl who was determined to change the world.

Altruistic humanitarian work is challenging and fraught with hardships but also fulfilling, bringing pure joy and deep satisfaction.

To truly Make a Difference in this troubled world is to gain a sense of empowerment rather than helplessness in the face of social injustice. To be useful, effective and achieve results – even small ones – will be the source of immense fulfilment and sense of Purpose.

I want to join with other humanitarians and community leaders to reduce suffering and increase joy. To find comrades in a worthy cause will be to forge the deepest friendships.

As I've said, when we get older, we have heartfelt emotional needs to be wanted and needed, respected and valued for our lifetime of experience. We have loads of love to give and there's a world out there desperate to be loved capable of returning the love in abundance. When I was almost 60, I was ready for that new life.

Ask yourself, what is your specialised knowledge, what are your unique skills and talents, and what vital resources can you share with those in need?

Gail Sheehy in New Passages writes: *"Experts in gerontology make a clear distinction between passive ageing and successful ageing. To engage in successful ageing is actually a career choice. Your job is to revive your life energy to make the next passage."*

Chapter 9

Empowerment Through Four H's

In the classic bestseller, *The 7 Habits of Highly Effective People*, Stephen Covey writes about being 'principle centred.'

"The ideal, of course, is to create one clear centre from which you consistently derive a high degree of security, guidance, wisdom, and power, empowering your proactivity and giving congruency and harmony to every part of your life."

"Principles do not change. We can depend on them. Principles don't react to anything…Principles are deep, fundamental truths, classic truths, generic common denominators. They are tightly interwoven threads running with exactness, consistency, beauty and strength through the fabric of life."

Reading Covey challenged me to ask myself: 'What are my principles? What are the fundamental truths I live by?' I realised my values are based on the four H's: *human needs, human rights, harm prevention*, and *healing*.

Through years of studying developmental psychology, I discovered that human needs are at the very core of understanding human nature.

As I matured, my thinking evolved to believe in the human rights of everyone to have their human needs met. I believe in doing no harm – a principle that runs through all religions and philosophies as the basis of ethics.

I am dedicated to the skills of problem-solving, decision-making and conflict-resolution to fulfil human needs, achieve human rights and prevent harm. And I believe in the necessity of healing where harm has occurred and the essential role of healers. With these principles as my foundation, I have embraced a model that can be taught in group workshops.

Exploring Human Needs

American Psychologist, Abraham Maslow (1908 – 1970) gave us the famous Hierarchy of Needs, with five tiers. At the base of the pyramid are *physiological* (survival) needs. Then we need *safety and security, love and belonging, esteem and respect for self and others*, and at the top of the pyramid, humans aspire to *self-actualisation*, which includes morality and creativity.

American Psychiatrist, William Glasser, (1925 - 2013) put his own spin on human needs, dividing them into five categories: *Survival, Love and Belonging, Power, Fun* and *Freedom*.

Glasser's *Survival* needs include physiological needs, as well as safety and security and health.

Love and Belonging encompasses the needs for a range of relationships including a life partner; family relationships between parents, children, siblings; friendships and belonging to community. I believe we can also include the need for relationships with God, nature and animals and the need for cultural and geographical belonging.

Relationships should meet emotional needs such as the need for bonding, intimacy, acceptance, approval, affection, attention, validation, recognition, respect, encouragement, support, trust, nurturing and protection. We are social beings like all mammals and need connection and interaction with others throughout life.

Glasser's concept of *Power* includes the human need to work and succeed, to gain mastery of knowledge and skills and impact the world; to be competent and capable of learning and achieving (rather than helpless and dependent.)

Glasser's word *Fun* might seem like a flippant human need. However, Fun encompasses all forms of creativity and cultural activities. And this need runs very deep from childhood, with the innate desire to build, create artwork, sing and play music, and tell stories, throughout our adult lives as we pursue inventive endeavours.

Glasser includes *Freedom* as a fundamental need, claiming that without freedom we cannot pursue our other needs. We need the freedom to think, feel and make our own decisions and act for ourselves. We need freedom of movement and freedom of expression. This is why imprisonment damages the human soul and tyranny crushes our essence of autonomy.

Protecting Human Rights

If human needs are so fundamental to survival and wellbeing, then we all have a birthright to meet these needs at every stage of life. In December, 1948, the United Nations launched the *Universal Declaration of Human Rights*. The historic document, created after the devastation of World War 2, contains 30 articles, starting with Article One: "All human beings are born free and equal in dignity and rights."

The declaration is the foundation of international human rights law and has inspired more than 80 international human rights treaties and declarations. It is the most translated document in the world with over 500 translations in different languages.

In claiming our own human rights, we also have *responsibilities* to protect and ensure the rights of others.

We cannot claim our rights at the expense of others. It's important to add that rights must also be extended to all animals and living creatures and our precious environment. All of us sharing Planet Earth have a right to live without harm and suffering.

Obstacles to Human Needs – Human Rights Abuses

As we go through life, other people or circumstances will obstruct the meeting of our needs. Others can cause harm and violate our need for safety and security, survival and health.

Poverty obstructs millions of people from having their basic survival needs met and being subjected to malnutrition and preventable diseases, deprivation, and daily suffering. Poverty is caused through the social injustice of inequality of wealth distribution.

The violence and destruction of war is a human rights violation on a mass scale. War is a crime against humanity. Crimes of assault, murder or theft are human rights violation against the individual.

Child abuse has four categories: *physical abuse, emotional abuse, sexual abuse* and *neglect* (a failure of caregivers to meet a child's needs). Children can be traumatised and damaged for life by these abuses.

Abuse, crime and human rights violations, in a multitude of forms, cause harm to humans, animals and the environment. These acts must be prevented. It's our job as caring, responsible people to protect others from harm.

As individuals, in all our relationships with family and friends and community we must respect and protect the rights of others. As members of society, we must identify and not ignore human rights violations and champion human rights for all.

Human rights must be the principle we operate from, regardless of political or religious differences.

Flawed beliefs and negative emotions are at the core of harmful actions. When individuals or organisations (such as governments, corporations, churches, and other institutions) embrace beliefs based on self-interest, and manipulate and exploit others, they cause immense harm.

In achieving social change, thought leaders of society must start with creating new belief systems – philosophy, policy and manifestos – as the foundation for positive actions. A progressive society must continually update belief systems based on current knowledge, not cling to outmoded traditional beliefs. For example, in solving the environmental crisis, we need an enlightened political system based on care of the planet rather than unrestricted economic growth.

Healing from Harm

When people have suffered harm through abuse and trauma, or grief and loss, they need healing through therapy, care, and support. Just as perpetrators of abuse also require healing, if rehabilitation is possible.

Human beings are resilient and can recover with understanding, empathy, kindness, compassion, forgiveness, and grace. It is our human responsibility and duty of care to provide healing for those who have suffered physical and or psychological abuse.

In the same way, animals and the natural world are resilient and can heal and regenerate if protected and nurtured and allowed to recover from damage.

I have a preference to work for prevention of harm and stopping harmful practices before they happen.

However, victims must be helped to recover by dedicated carers as we campaign together to eradicate all forms of abuse and violations of human rights, animal rights and environmental rights.

Together, we can create a fairer, safer, kinder world. Will you be part of creating a beautiful world for future generations?

In the words of Nelson Mandela: "To deny people their human rights is to challenge their very humanity."

Nelson Mandela, the famous South African anti-apartheid activist who was imprisoned for 27 years, became the first President of South Africa from 1994 to 1999.

Part Two

Choosing A Cause

Chapter 10

Recalling My Calling

In my soul searching at 57, in January 2014, I was gripped again with a passionate desire to Make a Difference to alleviate suffering. I had the good sense to know I couldn't take on every problem in our troubled world. I had to choose just one worthy cause.

I remembered that back in 1999, I read article in the *Australian Women's Weekly* that shocked me to the core. The riveting feature was about a famous Somalian model, Waris Dirie, who fled her homeland at the age of 12 when she was promised in marriage to an old man in exchange for five camels. The courageous little girl miraculously made it to London and worked as a servant.

When working as a shy teenager in McDonalds, she was discovered by a photographer and became, along with Naomi Campbell and Iman, one of the elegant black supermodels of the 80s. But her spectacular success is not the point of the story.

This beautiful young woman carried a hidden shame. Her first memory was being five years old and having her clitoris and labia sliced off with a blood-caked razor. Her mother held her down while the 'cutter' performed the agonising ritual. Waris recovered in a hut, her genitals sewn together with thorns, her legs bound.

This was the first time I'd ever heard of female circumcision or Female Genital Mutilation (FGM) and I was horrified. I bought Waris Dirie's autobiography, *Desert Flower* and pored over every captivating word about her extraordinary journey.

I wrote to the UN and asked for information and was sent a massive tome of documents by post. This was before advances with the internet. I learned everything I could about FGM. I made a vow that one day I would work to help stop this outrageous abuse of girls and women around the world.

So I found myself 14 years later, after my kids had grown into successful, happy adults, recalling that heartfelt vow made in 1999 and realised the time had arrived.

I discovered that Waris Dirie had become the United Nations Ambassador working to prevent FGM globally and had written three more books and launched the impressive *Desert Flower Foundation.*

I was off and racing, connecting with the Foundation, attending workshops, researching, and writing furiously, pitching stories to editors and reaching out to charities in the field. I immersed myself in disturbing facts and hopeful strategies to prevent the harmful practice. Knowledge is the necessary step before action.

I was invigorated. I had found my cause.

"All is possible when your heartfelt vision is in alignment with your values.

Believe in your dream, love it, breathe it, and let it fill your thoughts, but you must take action also.

Work towards it a little each day until it becomes your primary action.

Dreams are first envisaged but then they must be built.

You will succeed if you work at it."

Heart and Soul inspirational cards by Toni Carmine Salerno

Chapter 11

The Cruelest Cut of All

Some people might dismiss what is euphemistically called 'female circumcision' as a custom of other cultures that people in developed countries should accept as their right; a 'social norm' we should not judge or condemn.

However, if a sweet, innocent, adorable little toddler was wandering down the street, laughing and playing and was suddenly grabbed by a gang of thugs, dragged into the bushes, held down, and had her legs forced apart and her genitals sliced up, you would consider this a crime, the worst crime imaginable.

This violence against children is legislated as a crime in most countries. And yet, this atrocity is justified as a custom, a tradition, which outsiders must not interfere with.

The United Nations (UN) and World Health Organization (WHO) estimate that worldwide 8,000 girls a day, almost three million girls a year, are subjected to Female Genital Mutilation.

200 million women and girls are currently living with the consequences of FGM. A further 30 million girls are at risk of being cut in the next decade across 90 countries in Africa, the Middle East, Asia, and diaspora communities worldwide if the harmful practice is not stopped.

After FGM had been on the decline throughout Africa in recent years, the latest reports reveal that this horrific practice is on the rise again. 4.2 million girls are at risk of FGM in 2023 – more than ever before.

Even in the UK, it's estimated that 170,000 women are living with FGM, and 65,000 girls are at risk of being mutilated right here in the 'civilised' United Kingdom when migrants cling to this entrenched custom.

This brutal assault is not done by Whites to Blacks. It is done by Blacks to Blacks; specifically by black women on behalf of black men against little black girls, their own daughters. These mothers do not hate their daughters. They believe the cutting is an 'act of love' to ensure their daughters are 'clean' and marriageable. It is the mother who holds down the toddler while an old woman with a rusty razor blade, a knife, scissors, or piece of glass cuts into the delicate flesh of the terrified, screaming child, with no anaesthetic, causing excruciating pain and emotional trauma.

Many girls die of blood loss, shock and infection. If she survives, the traumatised child will be left with a raw wound where the clitoris and lips of her vagina have been cut off and in the case of 'infibulation', she has been sewn up leaving only a tiny hole.

A Lifetime of Pain

The reason for this barbarous cruelty? To preserve her virginity for marriage and to obliterate her sexual desires and the risk of infidelity to her future husband; to keep her pure, to ensure she experiences not pleasure, but abject pain with sexual intercourse, after she is cut open by the groom on her wedding night.

In many poor communities circumcised daughters command a high 'bride price' as mutilation and infibulation is meant to ensure virginity.

Ultimately, FGM is about power and control over female sexuality, which has become entrenched as a social norm in countless communities for generations.

For this enforced control, she will suffer health problems and pain her whole life. And emotional and psychological damage. Many African women are condemned to a lifetime of suffering every time they urinate and during menstruation, sexual intercourse, and childbirth.

The mutilation of her genitals means she has a high risk of complications when giving birth and could suffer obstetric fistula. This horrendous condition occurs during childbirth when the birth canal is torn leaving a hole in the wall of the vagina between the bladder or rectum. The woman will suffer leakage, leading to a life of shame and ostracism from her community, unless she has reparative surgery. Many circumcised women die giving birth because the scar tissue of the vagina has lost elasticity.

Unlike male circumcision, which cuts off loose skin on the penis, female circumcision cuts off flesh and removes part of the clitoris, a vital body organ, filled with highly sensitive nerve endings. Female circumcision is female castration. And castration is disempowering in every way.

How can African women ever be empowered to pursue education and work to transform communities alongside men, if they are maimed and suffer incapacitating pain their whole lives? How can women enjoy satisfying, loving sex lives with their husbands if they suffer pain, fear, and shame with intercourse? How can she feel self-esteem and pride in being a sexual woman?

Extreme Child Abuse

I watched the brilliant movie *Long Walk To Freedom* about the extraordinary life of revered leader, Nelson Mandela and the struggle of the South African people for freedom, equality and democracy. And yet for all the freedom fighting, sacrifice of lives and ultimate political victory, the atrocity of FGM against innocent children continues in the continent of Africa, (and other countries), tacitly sanctioned as a generational custom, with authorities turning a blind eye, even in countries where it is illegal.

In these days of easy access to information through the global reach of the internet, people around the world must be informed and take a stand against this widespread crime against children.

FGM is a specialised form of child abuse, a human rights abuse, a violation of humanity of the worst kind, and must be stopped urgently. Caring women and men around the world must help save the lives of millions of girls and stop the cruelest cut of all. We must also offer help to the 200 million victims of FGM by providing reparative surgery and emotional support to reclaim health, self-esteem, and empowerment.

In her book, *Desert Flower*, Waris Dirie writes: "All my life I've tried to think of a reason for my circumcision. Maybe if I could have thought of a good reason, I could accept what they'd done to me. But I could think of none.

"I feel that God made my body perfect the way I was born. Then man robbed me, took away my power, and left me a cripple. My womanhood was stolen. If God has wanted those body parts missing, why did he create them? I just pray that one day no woman will have to experience this pain. It will be a thing of the past."

Read Waris Dirie's inspirational books Desert Flower, Desert Dawn, Desert Children and Saving Safa and watch the movie, Desert Flower.

Chapter 12

Dispelling Myths

The white businessman joked: "The campaign to stop Female Genital Mutilation is a fight to Save the Clitoris!"

I was horrified and struck dumb! I wanted to retort: "Well, it's not about saving a body part. We are fighting to save little girls from the horrendous trauma of being deliberately maimed, which causes them to suffer for the rest of their lives."

Girls who are 'circumcised' at a young age – they can be defenceless babies or toddlers or sweet fun-loving kids of seven or eight or older – suffer shock, massive blood loss and infection that can kill them. If they survive the assault, they suffer chronic pain and health problems for the rest of their lives. Every time they wee is painful and from puberty, they suffer agony with every menstrual period.

When the girls are married off, the husband forces himself on his "pure, virginal bride" and sex is an agonising ordeal for her. Normal childbirth is painful enough, but for a circumcised woman childbirth is excruciating and the scarred birth canal risks multiple complications for the baby and mother.

In her book, *Saving Safa*, leading anti-FGM activist, Waris Dirie writes about her meeting with paediatrician, Dr Emma Acina who treats countless victims of FGM in her clinic in Djibouti.

Dr Acina says: "You can't imagine the awful injuries I see here every day: little girls with chronic inflammation of the vagina, bladder and kidneys; girls with tumours the size of tennis balls growing on scar tissue that just keep spreading; young women unable to pass urine and others whose mutilation has made them incontinent; young children who can't get a wink of sleep because of the pain."

The white woman at the conference quipped: "If you go to Africa to try to stop FGM you won't be popular with the men!"

Again, I was shocked and dumbstruck and floundered in my response. I wanted to express my indignation. "Don't you know anything about FGM! How could you trivialise this outrageous crime against innocent children!

My motivation to campaign against FGM is not about my *popularity!*

Happy Husbands

However, her uninformed comment got me thinking about the male perspective. Wouldn't a husband want a healthy, happy wife – a woman who had not had her vagina mutilated – who could enjoy making love and experiencing orgasm and sharing the pleasure of sex as part of a loving, equal, respectful relationship? Aren't there benefits for men too in saving women from this abuse? Loving sex should not be enmeshed with pain, female submission, and male dominance.

Some white academics theorise, ensconced in their ivory towers, that well-meaning 'outsiders' should not meddle with the customs of other cultures. This attitude makes me so furious I can barely speak. I want to say to these academics: "What if a culture had the custom to cut off a child's arm – to deliberately maim the child for life? Would we accept it as their right to practise this custom? Or, would we consider cutting off children's arms a shocking crime to be stopped at all costs?"

The passive attitude of acceptance is the stance of the Enabler on the Abuse Triangle; turning a blind eye to the Perpetrator's abuse of the Victim. There is no excuse or justification to accept or ignore harmful practices. Slicing off girls' genitals against their will is not some eccentric custom like body tattoos or piercings, which are personal choices and mostly harmless.

The Need for Intervention

FGM is a violent crime, extreme child abuse and a human rights violation that goes beyond a cultural custom. This atrocity is a global issue that demands 'outside' intervention to protect innocent children in the same way international charities intervene in countries in crisis by providing humanitarian aid.

The international community should not tolerate the harmful practices of insular cultures. When anyone breaks the law and commits what widespread humanity considers a crime (doing harm to another human being) we need Zero Tolerance.

We need top-down legislation that views FGM as a crime and condemns the custom, with legal consequences for perpetrators; the old women welding rusty razor blades and their accomplices who drag little girls from their beds into secret places to hold them down while she hacks away at tender flesh and then closes the wound with thorns.

To stop these acts of unimaginable cruelty, we also need a dynamic 'bottom-up' widespread education movement that works in villages at the grassroots level to challenge and change the 'social norms' that keep the practice going from one generation to the next.

We need intervention to break the generational cycle so that the trauma inflicted on the grandmother and mother is not inflicted on the daughter because cutting has been 'normalised' as something we have always done (as if tradition imbues abuse with dignity and merit.)

The way 'outside help' is given is important; not in a patronising, superior, forceful way but in an equal, respectful, collaborative partnership, where white women join with their black sisters, united as women (regardless of skin colour) and as human beings (regardless of nationalities and cultures) offering the benefits of the knowledge, skills, and resources we have to share to empower girls and women.

'Outsiders' from the developed world need to work alongside women in other cultures, in a respectful collaboration as equal partners in the cause, not in a rescuing and patronising way, to create deep and lasting cultural change. We need to change a collective mindset, which is not easy, but it is possible.

Challenging False Beliefs

Superstitions such as the belief that circumcision makes a girl clean, chaste and marriageable need to be challenged by rationality and education about female anatomy and the permanent damage to physical and mental health caused by FGM. We need to educate about human rights and gender politics, so families and communities learn to trust and respect their womenfolk and not attempt to control them out of shame of sexuality and fear of female empowerment.

Outsiders like me who are passionate about this cause want to empower women and men and children in Africa, the Middle East, Asia, and other countries where this atrocity is carried out.

We want to stop the shocking statistic of 8000 FGM victims a day from increasing. We want to end FGM and consign the harmful practice to the horrors of history.

The atrocity is embedded in the concrete of poverty. Charities, NGOs and governments must assist communities to break free from the injustice of poverty – to partner in food growing, supplying clean water and sanitation, decent housing, school for kids, jobs for men and women and medical facilities – the basics of life we all deserve – in villages across Africa and other under-resourced countries.

It must never be acceptable to maim little girls, so they are considered 'clean' to fetch a good 'bride price' from husbands. The enticement of a bride payment should not be the way to ease the burden of crushing poverty.

What really enrages me is that this lifelong disability is caused deliberately.

Parents everywhere experience a heart-breaking tragedy when their baby is born with an illness or disability and can blame the unfairness of fate.

However, when a child is deliberately maimed for life how can we comfort ourselves? Such a disability can be prevented. And it's up to you and me to be outraged and fired up to save innocent children from such indefensible cruelty.

FORWARD (Foundation for Women's Health, Research and Development) is the leading African women-led women's rights organisation working to end violence against women and girls. The organisation has been dedicated for more than 30 years to preventing female genital mutilation and child marriage and promoting maternal health in the UK and Africa.

Based in London, FORWARD has a beautiful Vision: *"We are working for the day when African girls and women will live in dignity, are healthy, have choices and enjoy equal rights free from fear of violence."*

The Girl Generation, based in Nairobi, Kenya is another dynamic organisation devoted to ending FGM, working closely with the *Orchid Project* and other partners.

Chapter 13

From Sceptic to Believer

I wrote this piece when I was in the process of researching strategies for stopping FGM; everything from legal prosecution and media campaigns to top-down education of villagers and providing safe houses for girls under threat of being cut.

When I read about using sponsorship to protect girls, at first, I was sceptical. *The Desert Flower Foundation* scheme of sponsoring a little girl by having a supporter pay a monthly donation to the girl's family to keep her safe from FGM, seemed like a blatant bribe, especially if the parents still believed in the cruel practice.

I have a strong opinion that is essential to transform the mindset of African families and communities to achieve real change. To stop this widespread crime requires a dynamic grassroots movement of educating women, men and children in every village across Africa and every country where FGM is a deeply-rooted custom. We need to dig it out by its poisonous roots.

Waris Dirie herself had similar doubts about sponsorship, expressed in her thought-provoking book *Saving Safa*.

Safa is the adorable little girl from Djibouti who played the role of Waris as a child in *Desert Flower*, the enthralling movie about her life, which was screened in cinemas in 2009, bringing to world attention the horrific crime of Female Genital Mutilation. The brilliant movie is available on YouTube and DVD.

The Desert Flower Foundation formed a contract with Safa's parents to provide on-going food supplies and necessities in exchange for a legal agreement that they would not subject their daughter to FGM.

Four years later, when Safa was seven, Waris received a letter from the courageous little girl expressing fear that she was at risk. Shocked and alarmed, Waris jumped on a plane to visit the family living in Balbala, an impoverished refugee slum on the outskirts of Djibouti city.

Safa's mother, Fozia revealed her true feelings in an outburst of rage: "We are shunned because we have an unclean, uncircumcised daughter. You know what happens to women who don't submit to the traditions. We have to live with this shame that you have laid upon us! Safa is an outsider. In our village and everywhere. We are all outsiders."

Waris sadly realised that the family cared more about being accepted and respected in the village than the health and happiness of their daughter.

And in a confrontation with Safa's obstinate father, Waris realised: "Idriss had shown his true colours when he said that his family needed the money and food the foundation provided every month. Safa's parents still weren't convinced of the cruelty and senselessness of female genital mutilation. They were sparing their daughter for purely economic reasons."

And this is the core of the issue. It is not effective to bribe poor families to spare their daughters if they are doing it for the wrong reasons: for money.

Such a cynical arrangement leads to resentment and the risk they will concede to community pressure.

Yes, we well-off folks must assist disadvantaged families by extricating them from the soul-destroying trap of poverty. Horrendous poverty is at the bitter heart of this entrenched abuse. Parents mutilate their daughters to make them 'clean and pure' and marriageable, so they fetch a good bride price.

Ignorance is also the heavy rock holding the custom in place from generation to generation. We, in the developed world, must partner with our African sisters and brothers, daughters and sons, to spread information about the dangers of FGM to eradicate distorted beliefs. We must also appeal to parents' love for their children; their natural instincts to nurture and protect their daughters from harm, pain and suffering.

Supporting Families

In the end Waris won over Safa's father, pulling him back from the brink of despair to realise there is hope for widespread change in his homeland through financial support of families along with dynamic education.

I am a convert. I now believe sponsorship has a vital role to play, so long as the support goes hand in hand with grassroots education about the horrors of FGM. And 'hand-outs' should be a starting point for empowering families and villages to become self-sustaining.

Here's why I believe the *Desert Flower Foundation* sponsorship scheme is worth supporting:

1. Sponsorship is an expedient, efficient, quick and easy way people in well-off countries can instantly help stop the atrocity of FGM. Not everyone can go to Africa to volunteer to spread the word. Not every individual can give a massive donation, but we can all make affordable, monthly payments.

2. Sponsoring one little girl and one family is very personal. You bond and connect and get to know and love your Sponsor Child and her family. Instead of generic charity, taking responsibility for just one little person makes your contribution very real.
3. I've had first-hand experience of sponsoring a child through Compassion. I started supporting Eyael, who lives in Ethiopia, when she was just eight until she grew into a beautiful young woman. I haven't missed the £20 per month and yet this small amount has transformed her life and eased her family's hardship. A lasting commitment to sponsorship really works.

While supporting sponsorship, my research led me to discover an exciting strategy that has saved hundreds of thousands of girls from harm and transformed villages across West Africa.

'My grandma circumcised a lot of girls in our house,' Safa confided in a near-whisper. 'The girls screamed just like I did in the film. But I didn't really know what she was doing.' My little Safa had been living under the same roof as a cutter-woman. Her own grandmother earned money by mutilating girls.

'Waris, said Safa, interrupting my thoughts. 'I'm so scared that one day they're going to circumcise me too.' She fell into my arms sobbing.

'Sweetheart,' I whispered, 'please trust me. I will protect you.'

From the book, *Saving Safa* by Waris Dirie.

Chapter 14

The Tostan Breakthrough

Everyone on Planet Earth who feels empathy and concern for the suffering of others agrees that the cruel and harmful practice of female genital mutilation must stop.

We all want to prevent the trauma, human rights violation and life-long suffering inflicted on innocent girls every day across Africa and around the world.

The real question is HOW do we stop this deeply entrenched custom that has continued for over 2,000 years, passed down from generation to generation, where a mother who has endured the trauma as a child inflicts the same trauma on her daughter? How do we break the generational cycle?

There's the legal approach. Governments have enacted laws against FGM and threatened "cutters" with imprisonment. And still they are defiant. The day the law was passed in Senegal in 1999, one village cut 100 girls in protest.

Another strategy is to target traditional cutters and give them alternative employment. However, mothers will still find someone to cut their daughters.

Another way is having anti-FGM activists host meetings in villages and lecture the women about the horrendous health consequences of slicing off a beautiful, precious child's genitals with a razor blade without anaesthetic. The older women are told that if the girl does not die from shock, blood loss or infection, she is condemned to a lifetime of pain and suffering.

And life is hard enough in poor rural villages in Africa without adding unnecessary hardship to the lives of women who carry the burden of childbirth, childcare and work.

Sadly, all heavy-handed, authoritarian methods have not stopped FGM. Shocking, shaming, blaming, judging, and condemning have failed abysmally to end the widespread harmful practice.

So WHY have these methods failed?

The 'tradition' is fiercely defended in African communities as a religious duty, a way to honour ancestors and to gain marriageability, family honour and respectability. And the practice is wrapped in a code of silence where women are forbidden to talk about the tradition they revere as a deeply personal and sacred rite of womanhood.

And yet, how long the tradition has existed, or the strength of feelings and beliefs doesn't make FGM right. For the health and wellbeing of millions of girls and women, the harmful practice must stop.

The Breakthrough

One courageous American woman has found a way. Through almost 50 years of living and working in Senegal, Molly Melching has devised a strategy that promises to end FGM across Africa and the world.

The exquisitely written book *However Long the Night* by author Aimee Molloy tells the inspirational story of Molly's journey from a bright-eyed university student from Illinois to a powerful campaigner heading up the acclaimed organisation, *Tostan*.

In the Senegalese language of Wolof, *tostan* is a beautiful word meaning the hatching of an egg at the breakthrough moment when the chick emerges from the shell.

Molly Melching hatched not just a good idea but gave birth to a human rights revolution. Since 1991, Tostan has led more than 9,500 communities in Senegal and other countries to make public declarations to end the practice of Female Genital *Cutting*. Tostan prefers to call the practice FGC rather than FGM. Millions of people have been reached and communities transformed through Tostan's remarkable work.

Tostan's grassroots movement to end FGC is now spreading throughout Africa with the potential to end the practice within a generation. This phenomenal achievement has come through a unique, pioneering approach.

What is the Secret to Tostan's Success?

Molly wanted to understand the motives driving the practice. Through talking with empathy and understanding with thousands of women in villages she discovered:

1. Mothers cut their daughters as *an act of love*. Cutting makes a daughter marriageable in a culture where women depend on husbands for their survival. An uncut woman would be unable to find a husband and become a social outcast, shunned and ridiculed as 'unclean' by other women. To cut her daughter makes her a respected member of the village, honours her family, and secures her future. Although misguided, the maternal intentions are *good*.
2. African culture is built on interconnectedness. Change cannot be made by individuals. If one girl or a few girls are spared from being cut, they risk ostracism and social disgrace.

Even if a whole village stops the practice, it is not enough because people are related to members of other villages; with relatives in at least 10 other surrounding villages. Change has to occur amongst all the villages in a region. Abandoning the practice must be a collective decision.

3. Abandoning the tradition cannot be done through force or shame, or patronising judgement. Stopping FGC must be done with respect and understanding of the beliefs and fears, motives, and social needs of the people through equal, collaborative discussion.
4. The continuation of the tradition is based on ignorance and misinformation. Women attribute the pain and health problems experienced by girls and women to bad spirits. They have not connected haemorrhaging, infection, and death of girls to the cutting procedure. Nor do they know that suffering pain in urination, menstruation, sexual intercourse, and childbirth is not normal. They believe such pain is part of being a woman; that every woman suffers in the same way. They believe that cutting girls is normal and universal; that all women around the world are cut.

Through Tostan's educational workshops in remote rural villages women have become hungry for knowledge and discovered empowerment.

Tostan's Three-part Approach to Transformation

1. **Health Education:** Knowledge about anatomy and health given in a respectful participatory way using creative means such as theatre, music and dance with women sharing their stories has broken through the code of silence, myths, and mistaken beliefs to confront the harmful effects of cutting girls.

2. **Human Rights:** Informing women that they have a right to a free choice about what's done to their bodies, a right to health, to live without pain and to experience sexual pleasure has changed attitudes and lives. Teaching human rights has stopped FGC as well as child marriage and domestic violence and has empowered women to take on leadership roles in their villages.
3. **Public Declaration:** Villages have come together to make public declarations to end FGC, which has ensured the power of collective commitment and accountability. The entire community mindset has been changed, not just isolated cases of non-conformity, with the risk of ostracism.

Bringing the harmful practice out in the open has broken the code of secrecy and created unity and powerful resolve amongst men and women, boys and girls.

Tostan has led an astonishing human rights revolution and the movement will continue until every girl is safe to grow up happy and healthy.

Be inspired: read Molly's remarkable life story, *However Long The Night*. Visit the Tostan website and become a supporter. *The Orchid Project,* based in London, supports the revolutionary work of *Tostan* throughout Africa and the world.

In Molly Melching's inspiring biography, author, Aimee Molloy, quotes Molly as saying: *"I want to be remembered most for having made empowering education – particularly knowledge of human rights and responsibilities – accessible to millions of people at the grassroots level, helping them achieve their full potential."*

Chapter 15

This is Personal

I was a happy little girl, brimming with joy (that was my middle name), curiosity ('How did those daffodils suddenly appear out of the ground?') and trust (I believed I could rely on grown-ups to look after me).

At seven in Grade Two I could cover my own exercise books; first the brown paper, neat corners, sticky tape, then a cheerful picture from an old greeting card stuck on with clag and finally a layer of smooth plastic. I was so good at this, my friend Leonie wanted me to cover her books too. That made me incredibly pleased with myself.

I was bursting with anticipation for Old Miss McConky to read another chapter of *The Magic Faraway Tree* every afternoon. One sunny day after school Cheryl asked me to go to her house because she had some nail polish. We could paint our nails. I'd never done that before!

Giggling with excitement we raced across the park. But my secure little life was about to change. I was about to lose my innocence. There was a man in a car driving really slowly and smiling at me. At ME! Not Cheryl! It was ME he liked. And I smiled back, blonde fringe and dimples and pretty dress.

That was the day I was molested by a stranger; the day I started to believe I was dirty and there was something wrong with me. It was my secret. I was a good girl on the outside, but I was bad inside, full of guilt, full of shame. It was my fault because I was so silly to get in his car. And then there were the nightmares. He was coming through the window to kill me with a knife, or a gun. I would scream and climb into bed with mum, sobbing and trembling.

I Understand Childhood Trauma

This is why I understand and empathise, with every fibre of my being, what it's like to be a happy little girl skipping along enjoying childhood innocence and then suddenly one act, just one single trauma, changes you, shames you, forever.

The little girl in Africa, dark skin, tight curls, beautiful smile, big brown eyes, is dancing through the desert dust to class to learn and sing and laugh. After school she helps her mummy make family meals and plays with her pet goat. One day this sweet child is taken to a terrifying secret place, held down, her tiny legs are forced apart and her tender parts sliced off with a razor blade, blood gushing, the wound sealed with thorns, the pain swamps her body and crushes her heart, destroying her trust forever.

In this troubled world, there are so many problems to solve, so much cruelty to stop, so many worthy causes to champion. Which one will I choose? The issue of female genital mutilation breaks my heart and outrages my mind because I was once an innocent little girl who suffered a life-changing trauma too.

My experience of being molested was traumatic but doesn't compare in magnitude to the extreme trauma of being mutilated. If the little African girl survives the shock, the blood loss and infection, she will suffer for the rest of her life; every time she wees it hurts, and later, every time she menstruates is agony.

Having sex with her husband will be excruciating, not pleasure. And childbirth; a horrendous, life-threatened ordeal.

More than 200 million women around the world live with the post-traumatic emotional and physical damage of being mutilated as children. This is a cause that demands attention. Our genitals are meant to be a source of pleasure and power; the pleasure of lovemaking and the power to create new life. Female empowerment depends on stopping this violent crime.

I Understand Pain

There's another reason I can relate to this disturbing issue, even though I'm a pale-faced, mature-aged woman who grew up in suburban Australia and now living in rural England, not a remote village in Somalia, Ethiopia, Uganda, Sudan, or Kenya.

For 12 years, after giving birth to my second child, I suffered undiagnosed endometriosis. Every month I was incapacitated with overwhelming menstrual pain until a hysterectomy at 44 ended my roller coaster of suffering.

Now I want to join the fight to stop the needless suffering of other women because a lifetime of pain is preventable. Empowerment is possible. The empowerment of future generations of women all over the world begins with the end of this widespread, disempowering abuse. Of all the worthy causes in this troubled world, stopping FGM is a cause worth fighting for.

Will you join the fight to protect innocent little girls from one of the worst form of child abuse?

"Childhood trauma affects our later experiences, and who we become as an adult. It spoils the blueprint of our natural developmental stages, hijacks our brain, mind and body, and shapes our perceptions, expectations and reactions. It cloaks us in a shadow of shame, self-doubt, guilt, self-blame, disempowerment, and mistrust. The many symptoms of PTSD and Chronic/childhood-PTSD fragment all aspects of our lives. We have inner wounds that never fully heal. We feel damaged and irreparable, and we spend much of our time and energy trying to hide this from those who might judge or reject us."

Maxine Harley, MSc Integrative Psychotherapy, specialises in recovery from childhood trauma. She is the Author of two books and a series of self-help guides for healing the effects of inner child wounding available on maxineharley.com

Chapter 16

The Ultimate Feminist Issue

The mother of feminism, the provocative author of the 1970 classic, *The Female Eunuch*, the eternally controversial Germaine Greer has missed the most important feminist issue of our times.

Victims of female genital mutilation have suffered actual, not figurative, castration. The 200 million women around the world who have been subjected to this horrific abuse are the real Female Eunuchs.

The word 'eunuch' refers to men who have been castrated by having their testicles (and sometimes the penis) cut off. It was a cruel practice first inflicted by rulers in ancient civilisations to create impotent, docile servants and has continued for centuries as a means of subjugation.

Castration means removal of the testicles, where the male sex hormone, testosterone and sperm are produced. Male cattle, horses, dogs, and other domesticated animals are castrated to make them infertile.

Boys have also been castrated in Italian operatic circles, to keep their singing voices in the upper register. These castrated boys are often called eunuchs or 'castrati'.

Castration can occur by accident such as war injuries, pelvic crushing from car crashes or severe burns. Or sadly, the loss of testicles can happen through surgery for medical conditions such as testicular cancer or prostate cancer. This cruelty has been inflicted on males as a form of torture, punishment, or self-mutilation.

With the rise of transgenderism, male to female gender reassignment surgery, involving removing the testicles, is becoming more common. 'Vaginoplasty' is a surgical procedure to create a vagina and vulva from a man's genitals. In female to male surgery, women have surgery to create a penis, remove their breasts and taking high doses of testosterone to become a 'man'.

Regarding male circumcision, medical experts agree that cutting off the foreskin of the penises of babies and boys is an unnecessary and painful procedure. The foreskin is meant to protect the head of the penis.

There's a strong argument for leaving the genitals of females and males the way they were exquisitely designed.

Shock Value

Clever Germaine Greer hijacked the word 'eunuch' for the title of her iconoclastic book to refer to docile, disempowered women in the Western world; socially conditioned females who are pale imitations of men. In typical Greer style she used the term 'female eunuch' for maximum shock value for complacent readers in rich countries.

However, did our revered feminist scholar miss the tragic irony? The widespread practice of cutting off the clitoris and labia of little girls throughout Africa, the Middle East, Asia, and many other countries is a reality, not a literary device.

These real-life female eunuchs have had their womanhood and sexuality damaged so they experience no sexual pleasure or orgasm. They live with the memory of the trauma. They are permanently maimed and truly disempowered.

These 'cut' women require feminists' passionate attention; the perpetrators require feminists' outrage and the 8,000 innocent girls at risk of FGM every day require feminists' fierce protection.

While feminists in the developed world debate issues of equal pay, workplace harassment, the glass ceiling and female CEOs in the boardroom, women across Africa, Asia, the Middle East not only face each day without the basics of enough food, clean water, sanitation, education, and jobs, they suffer continual pain from having their genitals mutilated as children.

Germain Greer, in her foreward to the 1991 edition of her provocative book that rocked the world in 1970, admits: "*The Female Eunuch* does not deal with poor women (for when I wrote it I did not know them) but with the women of the rich world, whose oppression is seen by poor women as freedom."

Real Feminism

Stopping FGM is a feminist issue worth fighting for. There are many other real feminist issues in poor countries such as sex slavery where young girls are forced into prostitution and used and abused; child marriage where young girls are forced to marry and have sex with old men; child labour and slave labour producing all those shiny consumer goods so cheaply available in the privileged part of the world. These human rights abuses are built on abject poverty and deprivation, where governments and corporations and the legal system turn a blind eye.

Other human rights abuses inflicted on women deny women freedom of speech, movement, dress, sexuality, ownership, education, and employment. This kind of oppression and control by men in certain cultures is based on a sinister power over women. Subjugation by the patriarchy.

Disturbing Facts

The ultimate abuse against humanity is war. The horrors of war are the invention by the powerful to kill and harm the innocent for profit. Weapons of war are big business. For centuries, billions of people have been killed and maimed, and generations of families traumatised by grief. Innocent young men in their prime have been slaughtered on gory battlefields because old men in power give orders from the safety of their mansions.

The brilliant book, *Half the Sky* is the new feminist manifesto. Authors, Nicholas D Kristof and Scheryl Wudunn, explore in depth how men in power exploit, control and abuse the impoverished women and children of the world.

After extensive research, the authors claim: "In the 19th century the central moral challenge we faced was slavery. In the 20th it was the battle against totalitarianism. In the 21st century it is the struggle for equality for women and their daughters around the world."

Half the Sky reveals some mind-boggling statistics: "More girls have been killed in the last 50 years, precisely because they were girls, than men were killed in all the battles of the 20th century. More girls are killed in this routine 'gendercide' in any one decade than people were slaughtered in all the genocides of the 20th century."

The authors identify three main abuses: sex trafficking and forced prostitution, gender-based violence such as honour killing and mass rape and the crime of FGM and maternal mortality, which claims the life of one woman every minute.

"One million children are forced into prostitution every year and the total number of prostituted children could be as high as 10 million. They are held captive and used by vicious pimps as sex slaves.

"Gender-based violence is ubiquitous in the developing world, inflicting more casualties than war, cancer, malaria and other diseases combined. Rape of teenage girls is a tradition in Africa, used to shame, humiliate and control.

"It is common in Asia for men to throw sulphuric acid in the face of girls or women who spurn them. The acid melts the skin and bones and if it hits the eyes will blind her. This is the depth of misogyny that keeps women living in fear and oppression.

"Violating a daughter by gang rape is used to punish a whole family in the Middle East. Or sometimes it takes the form of honour killing, in which a family kills one of its own girls because she has behaved immodestly or fallen in love with a man…the paradox of honour killings is that societies with the most rigid moral codes end up sanctioning behaviour that is supremely immoral: murder."

Obstetric fistula is another widespread affliction for women across Africa. "No one can fathom the sadistic cruelty of soldiers who use sticks to tear apart a woman's insides.

"But there is a milder, more diffuse cruelty of indifference, and it is global indifference that leaves some three million women suffering fistulas due to rape and obstructed labour and lack of medical care during childbirth."

Half the Sky is a catalogue of horrors inflicted on women and it makes tough reading. However, the book is infused with hope and optimism outlining inspiring success stories of women saved through humanitarian medical care and empowered through education, and freed from poverty and misogyny, cruelty and oppression.

Right at the outset of this astonishing book, the authors are transparent, writing this plea: "We hope to recruit you to join an incipient movement to emancipate women and fight global poverty by unlocking women's power as economic catalysts."

I have signed up to join the fight against these horrendous issues, starting with the ultimate feminist issue, the one the Mother of Feminism missed: stopping the crime of female eunuchs. When we stop FGM we will empower women and empowered women will change the world.

"When racism and sexism collide, feminists call it the theory of intersectionality, but for black women it's just known as Monday, Tuesday, Wednesday..."

Pontso Malethe, Comic Relief

Chapter 17

Challenging Social Norms

Tragic Lack of Knowledge

While most Africans throughout the 54 countries on this vast continent are either Muslim or Christian, the majority are also deeply Animist, with a belief in the ever-present spirit world; believing that bad spirits cause sickness, death, natural disasters and social calamities.

The human mind seeks out the cause of problems. Across cultures, all people try to understand why bad stuff happens. We all want someone or something to blame when tragedy strikes. However, without scientific knowledge explained in their own language, African cultures attribute all kinds of misfortune to malevolent spirits.

When a little girl dies after being cut by an old razor blade, the grief-stricken family and the whole community blame bad spirits, seeing no connection between the 'practice' and her death. They do not know about germ transmission and infection, the danger of excessive blood loss and the impact of shock and trauma.

Many girls die from the horrendous ordeal and those who survive are condemned to a lifetime of needless suffering. Every time they urinate and menstruate is painful, while intercourse and childbirth are agonising and fraught with complications.

An Act of Horror Motivated by Love

While the act of cutting girls' genitals is horrifying to outsiders, to communities throughout Africa, the practice is performed by women and encouraged by mothers as 'an act of love'.

This loving motivation by mothers was the profound discovery made by American community educator, Molly Melching during many years of living closely with villagers throughout Senegal.

Molly was able to see the practice of genital cutting through the eyes of understanding and compassion, rather than outrage and condemnation.

Molly's compassionate approach to educating villagers about the dangers of female genital cutting has been phenomenally successful in stopping the harmful practice throughout West Africa.

Her internationally acclaimed charity, Tostan has succeeded in reaching more than 9500 African communities and saving many thousands of girls from the trauma and lifelong damage of FGC since 1991. The UK charity, the Orchid Project is a staunch supporter of Tostan's great work.

How Do We Challenge False Beliefs and Social Norms?

Mothers believe that the ritual of cutting will ensure their daughters will be clean, chaste, virginal, marriageable, faithful to their husbands and accepted within the community. An uncut girl risks being shunned, ostracised and unmarried, which is a shameful and life-threatening fate.

Beliefs become embedded and unquestioned and passed down the generations as 'social norms'.

In the same way, in our Western culture we are conditioned to conform to all kinds of harmful behaviours that are accepted as normal: drinking alcohol, taking drugs, eating junk food, eating animals, watching pornography and violent movies, going to war, gambling, over-spending, obsessively engaging in social media, getting tattoos, body piercings and cosmetic surgery. We in developed countries are also victims of 'social norms' and non-conformists can be treated as misfits.

Social norms are prescribed behaviours practised by a group and they continue when they go unquestioned and are held in place by positive and negative sanctions. When someone conforms to a collective behaviour, they are rewarded and if they do not conform, they are socially punished with disapproval and rejection.

The intricacies of social norms perpetuate the harmful practice of female genital cutting. As Molly Melching discovered in her extensive research in villages throughout Senegal, the only way to stop the harmful practice is by breaking the social norm through education of local people, in their own languages, taught by facilitators from their own communities, in a respectful, non-judgemental way.

She explains that people will not stop this harmful practice that's been passed down through the generations for over 2,000 years, by being bullied or threatened by outsiders or even the law.

The Power of Information

Molly understands that remote communities need access to information about health and human rights and the stimulus and freedom to question the logic of beliefs for themselves in safe, trusting discussion groups and make their own connections, discoveries and insights. I agree. From my years of experience in therapy groups, I know that this is how we all learn, grow and change.

Tostan's Community Empowerment Program comprises classes of 25-30 participants, held twice a week, covering three comprehensive modules on health and human rights, spread over three years. In these dynamic classes, women, men and youth in remote rural villages sit in circles and explore and question deeply-held beliefs.

Disputing False Beliefs

The Belief that Cutting Makes a Girl 'Marriageable'

In a culture where a woman and her children are financially dependent on her husband for survival, a girl's family must ensure she is deemed marriageable and suitable to gain a Bride Price from the groom's family.

Mothers claim that the scar tissue from cutting off the labia makes the vagina look 'smooth and neat'. This subjective, aesthetic preference can be disputed so the natural vagina is seen as clean, neat, and correct. The idea that a 'cut girl' is attractive and desirable to a potential husband is a distorted belief. She is beautiful when she is intact, the way her body was designed to be.

A woman does not need to marry to be valuable. She can be educated, skilled and employed and independent and single if she chooses. However, most African girls want to get married because family is cherished. They're learning they don't have to marry young; they can get an education and aspire to more in life.

Increasingly, an African wife is no longer financially dependent on a husband.

Women in African villages generate income through small businesses, growing food and managing sustainable projects. Marrying off young daughters is not essential for a family's income. It is far better for the girl's future to stay at school and gain an education and qualifications, than marry when she's young and immature.

The Belief that Cutting Makes a Girl and Woman 'Clean'

Ironically, with the health and hygiene problems FGC creates, the opposite is true. Cutting causes problems with urination, periods, intercourse and childbirth, chronic infections, and the risk of obstetric fistula during a protracted labour, which damages the vaginal wall causing leakage from the rectum or bladder. Tragically, a woman suffering obstetric fistula is condemned as 'unclean' and shunned and ostracised by her community.

When women talk about these health issues, they realise these problems are not normal, but the result of being cut. They start to claim the right to health and wellbeing for their daughters.

The Belief that Cutting Guarantees a Girl's Virginity on her Wedding and Faithfulness throughout Marriage

A girl with knowledge about sex is empowered to say 'No' to boys and can choose to keep herself chaste through her own values. A wife can choose to be faithful when she is loved and respected by her husband.

Why is virginity and fidelity important to a husband? It seems to me that men want to protect themselves from the pain and shame of a wife's infidelity (and ensure the children are his). Men deflect pain and shame onto women and women carry a heavy load of physical and emotional pain and suffering about sexuality.

These male attitudes are steeped in hypocrisy, in my opinion, as the Muslim religion allows a man to have up to four wives.

A man can have several sexual partners and his wives are forced to endure jealousy, rivalry and being displaced by younger wives, as they get older.

When these relationship issues come under scrutiny in discussion groups, women and men understand how nonsensical and unfair the old beliefs are.

The Belief that Female Sexual Pleasure is 'Dangerous'

Many Africans believe that unless her clitoris is cut out, a woman can't control her sexual urges and would become wild and promiscuous. I think this belief is a projection of male lack of self-control, a way of blaming women for their own intense sexual feelings they don't understand. The female libido is not dangerous and evil. Such false beliefs must be challenged and a healthy attitude to sex discussed in a factual way amongst adolescent girls and boys.

FGC robs a woman of sexual pleasure and orgasm. This is a terrible loss and violation of a woman's right to a beautiful experience. Instead of pleasure, she experiences pain during intercourse and in all her reproductive functions. Women subjected to Type Three infibulation are sewn up to leave just a tiny hole and must be cut open on their wedding night, making first-time sex agonising.

The fact that sex is painful for women supports polygamy, as a wife can be relieved of her duty on some nights by other wives.

Women have a right to enjoy sexual pleasure, sensuality, and romance in their relationships. When women are not subjected to FGC, they discover that sexual desires are positive in a committed, caring marriage. Sexual pleasure is good for both husband and wife. Sexual enjoyment enhances attachment and emotional bonding, which leads to loyalty and devotion and a happy marriage and happy life for both a man and woman.

A man benefits from having a woman who enjoys sex, rather than suffers pain during intercourse. The idea that sex can be pleasurable for both husband and wife and that his wife's pleasure is beneficial for the man as much as her is a radical new concept for villagers in the Tostan program. When adolescent boys and men learn about the pain and suffering inflicted on girls and women through genital cutting, they usually become committed to stopping the practice.

A Culture Confused about Sexuality

In many African countries on local TV on Sunday morning, some channels have church services and gospel singing while other channels have music shows with explicit, soft porn music and dance videos, representing the two conflicting forces in the African psyche.

The British missionaries last century introduced prudish attitudes and Christian prohibitions on sex outside marriage. Puritanical views now co-exist with the African hearty sexual appetite.

Universally men and women need to embrace healthy sexuality, without confusion, shame and fear. Education in villages is helping communities understand that a loving – not forced - marriage can be good, a true blessing and foundation for a happy family and life together.

The Free Choice to Marry

Marriage needs to be at the right time, at the right stage of life – when a girl has grown into a mature woman, not when she is a child, as this is a form of abuse.

A young woman needs to be able to marry a man of her

choice; a loving, caring, compatible man of a similar age, not an old man. And the couple can learn how to have an equal, respectful, loving marriage and enjoy sexual intimacy and affection.

Girls and women must be protected from the trauma, agony and tyranny of genital cutting. They have a human right to be whole and healthy and enjoy loving sexuality. Stopping female genital cutting is essential to the empowerment for girls and women around the world.

As my avid research progressed, my personal commitment to this cause grew like wildfire. Finally, I had enough knowledge on this disturbing subject and was ready to grasp the nettle and take action. That's exactly what happened next.

"Knowledge is power. Information is liberating. Education is the premise of progress, in every society, in every family."

Kofi Annan

Secretary-General of the United Nations, 1997 – 2006.

Part Three

Taking Action

Chapter 18

This is the Beginning

I enrolled in the Tostan training course in Senegal, West Africa and was due to set off in July 2016. I wrote this blog post with a mixture of excitement and trepidation.

I'm going on a journey into the unknown and I want you, my readers, to join me as I face challenges and miracles. I'm not climbing Kilimanjaro or hiking the Pacific Crest Trail. My journey is not as physically gruelling as those heroic feats. Mine is a journey of the mind and heart; a journey with a goal, not for personal achievement, but to contribute to others.

I am documenting my journey in this blog I'm calling *Humanity Matters*. Throughout my career as a journalist, I've written about what matters; Family Matters, Relationship Matters, Health Matters, Travel Matters, Midlife Matters. And all these subjects really did matter at different stages of my life.

However, as I approach 60, I've arrived at a vantage point where one subject concerns me deeply and urgently: the suffering of humanity. I am gripped by a passionate desire to work to reduce suffering and increase joy, reduce abuse and increase love, reduce deprivation and increase prosperity.

I want to live a life of purpose and meaning, and I want to Make a Difference - a positive one – to the lives of others. When this desire took hold five years ago, I lacked focus.

I did some volunteer work in Ghana in 2012. My efforts were well intentioned but generalised and undirected. There are so many worthy causes and charities to work for, I wanted to embrace them all.

Then two years later I started asking myself the question, 'If I could pick one worthy cause to champion, what would it be?' And 'Bingo' I got the answer.

I've long been horrified by the shocking human rights violation, the vicious crime against the innocent, the ultimate form of child abuse – the deliberate maiming of millions of little girls through the practice of female genital mutilation (FGM).

I researched and wrote about the subject for over two years to understand the complex issues and to discover the most effective way to put an end to an entrenched custom that dates back 2,000 years that condemns little girls to an unimaginable trauma and a lifetime of pain and suffering.

That's when I discovered the work of pioneering American educator Molly Melching, who while living in Senegal for many years developed an innovative program of empowerment for girls and women. Her work, through the charity *Tostan*, is so successful; I want to join her team to introduce the life-changing program across Africa.

And I am inspired. I want to stop FGM – not just from a safe distance – but on the ground – in the country where a rusty razor blade is used on tender flesh on a daily basis.

A New Journey

And so I am setting off on a journey next week – a courageous one - to Senegal in West Africa to be trained in Molly's method with the big dream of taking the Tostan program to remote villages throughout East Africa.

This is a heavy, disturbing issue and it would be easy to feel outraged with anger and bitterness that fuel a fire in the belly *against* this child abuse and the old women who inflict it, the mothers who allow it and the patriarchal social system that demands that 'brides be clean'.

However, I would rather be motivated by conviction; to be inspired by what I stand for, which promotes value (while anger devalues). And what I stand for is *empowering women in Africa; human rights and social justice; protecting children; humanitarian work and compassion and kindness.*

Do you stand for these values? Will you join me on my journey of discovery because Humanity Matters; it really does.

"Develop enough courage so that you can stand up for yourself and then stand up for somebody else. Have enough courage to love. History, despite its wrenching pain, cannot be unlived, but if faced with courage, need not be lived again."

Maya Angelou, African-American Writer and Civil Rights Activist, (1928 – 2014)

Chapter 19

Training in Transformation

I wrote this article in 2016 so all dates, time frames and figures are true for this year.

When Molly made the profound statement: "This is a movement for social change. We are building critical mass," a wave of exhilaration swept through me, from head to toe.

Being part of this transformative grassroots movement across Africa is the culmination of my life experience. My diverse career in journalism, my endless studies in psychology and my decades of devotion to raising children has steered me along a meandering track but now I've returned to my core values and, quite possibly, the work I was born to do.

Having the purpose of improving the quality of life for the poorest of the poor fills me with joy, love and empowerment. Ever since I was an idealistic university student in my early 20s, the struggle for human rights and social justice lit a fire in my belly.

So here I am, sitting in a circle with a dream team of dedicated Tostan staff – Molly, Yussuf, Marmie, Birima, and our skilful translator, Cherif - and 23 other eager participants from around the world: America, England, Australia, Denmark, India, Morocco, Senegal, Gambia, Guinea-Bissau, Sierra Leone, Nigeria, Swaziland, Kenya, Uganda, and Tanzania.

A Celebration of Diversity

What a colourful mixture of cultures we are and yet we are united by a passion to make a difference. We've all come to this large round room, styled on an African thatch-roofed hut, at the impressive training centre and accommodation based in Thies, the fourth largest city of Senegal, two hours sultry drive from the bustling capital of Dakar to be trained in the Tostan method of community-led development.

'Tostan' in the national language of Wolof is an evocative word meaning 'breakthrough', the breaking of an egg, when the little chick emerges to start a new life. This unique program has been the catalyst for spreading transformation, indeed giving hope and new life to a multitude of resource-poor communities.

The dynamic organisation is celebrating its 25th anniversary this year, bringing education about health and human rights to hundreds of remote villages throughout West Africa, transforming life for millions of women, men, and children.

The fertile seeds of knowledge have miraculously sprouted life-enhancing projects in food production, clean water and sanitation, healthcare, schools, solar power, and income-generating projects such as tie-dying fabric, soap making, poultry farming and the greatest achievement of all, ending the harmful practice of female genital cutting (FGC) and child marriage of precious young girls.

Tostan Founder and CEO, Molly Melching is a pioneer with the rare combination of strength and tough determination mixed with the softness of empathy and compassion that comes from years of witnessing gruelling hardship and brutal deprivation and misery.

An America raised in the conservative midwestern state of Illinois, Molly, as an adventurous 24-year-old exchange student, landed in Senegal in 1974 for a six-month stint of studying African Literature at the University of Dakar. That was 42 years ago and she's still living in her beloved Senegal, with a fierce devotion to the Senegalese people.

Devotion to A Cause

Her devotion to Senegal led Molly to master fluent French (spoken by around 10 per cent of the population) and the national language of Wolof. There are 36 languages spoken throughout Senegal. Molly immersed herself in the culture by living in villages and truly understanding the people and their needs and aspirations through a process of non-judgemental, respectful 'deep listening'.

She came to understand that ignorance, or simply a dire lack of basic information, was at the root of so much unnecessary suffering. Without scientific explanations in their own language, villagers often attributed the cause of sickness, death, and misfortunes to 'bad spirits'.

She realised that knowledge is the key to empowerment; knowledge about good governance, health, anatomy, hygiene and germ-transmission, child development, human rights, problem solving and conflict resolution.

Through years of patient, compassionate listening to the locals' heartfelt values, yearning aspirations and deep desire for community wellbeing, Molly developed a comprehensive (some 2,000 pages) education program to be taught by local village facilitators in their own languages spread over three years.

Other well-meaning charities, NGOs and government agencies have often swept into poor communities, identified needs and imposed solutions, which were doomed to fail. In contrast, Molly's radical approach was to empower villagers with essential knowledge and allow them to join the dots, make their own connections, experience the thrill of light bulb moments and discover for themselves their needs and solutions. And the approach worked!

Tostan's transformative *Community Empowerment Program* (CEP) has been so successful, it's attracted funding and support from UNICEF, UNFPA, the Bill and Melinda Gates Foundation, the Carter Center, Hillary Clinton, the London-based Orchid Project and hundreds of loyal donors. The program's been scrutinised by curious academics, monitored and evaluated and won numerous prestigious awards including the Conrad N. Hilton Humanitarian Prize for 'extraordinary contributions toward alleviating human suffering.'

Rocket Launcher for Social Change

Once we human beings discover profound truth, we can't 'unknow' these facts. And this potent knowledge fuels the rocket launcher for unstoppable social change. With Tostan's guidance, village participants organised themselves into Community Management Committees (CMC) with enthusiastic elected representatives (over half of whom are women) meeting regularly to discuss problems and initiate creative projects. Village representatives also began gathering at monthly regional meetings that have now become a political force.

During our training CMC members joined our circle to share their experiences. The women, resplendent in their beautiful African dresses and headscarves, were once shy and silent and now travel by horse and cart from village to village as dynamic awareness-raising activists and respected leaders in their communities. We were also honoured to listen to an esteemed Imam explain how FGC is not condoned by the Muslim faith.

We were delighted to visit two villages in the district that have been working with Tostan for several years: the Village of Keur_Simbara and Keur_Thiem Saware.

I will always remember the warm, jubilant welcome as beautiful women and men in their colourful clothes and laughing children lined our path and clapped, drummed, danced, and sang as we arrived to join their gathering. We heard proud reports of their amazing projects and watched touching performances about all they had learned about human rights.

Our 10-day training course was enriched with singing, dancing, theatre and animated discussions and full-on participation in the same practical, hands-on ways villagers learn new information and skills.

For someone like me who usually sits in a workshop passively listening to the instructor and scribbling notes, I was gently pushed out of my comfort zone to brainstorm and perform on the spot! What a powerful way to learn! I've absorbed the knowledge deeply into my whole being, anchored by vivid memories.

In between sessions, we enjoyed scrumptious traditional meals served by elegant Senegalese ladies in the cool, spacious dining room where the effusive conversation bubbled over the spicy dishes as we shared stories and ideas!

A Plan of Action

On the final day we all presented our action plans to the group. I teamed up with lovely Millicent, an experienced Health Educator from Kenya, and together we created a vision for bringing the Tostan Empowerment Program to the remote rural communities where she lives.

In the Gratitude Circle, the hugs of affection between everyone were genuine and heartfelt and tears of love and appreciation flowed freely.

Pure Joy

By the time the farewell dinner celebration came around, we had all bonded and become good friends. Wearing our colourful African boubous and kaftans, each of us in turn danced across the hall with sheer exuberance and elation to music from our country of birth to receive certificates from Molly and Birima. Young Daniel and I busted some very unusual moves for Australia and had everyone in fits of laughter!

And then we exchanged gifts with our brothers and sisters from different countries, extending the hands of friendship and solidarity across the world.

My new sister, Nomcebo presented me with a stunning traditional shawl from Swaziland and I gave her a pretty floral plate and chocolates from the little English village of Tenterden in Kent, where I live.

These genuine friendships confirm that humanity is one big family. We are all the same – Birthplace: Earth, Race: Human, Politics: Freedom, Religion: Love.

An Inspiring Mentor

And spontaneously, as a fitting finale, our impromptu 'African Women's Choir' sang a rousing verse of *You Raise Me Up* to Molly Melching. She is a fearless champion of social change, who has become our inspiring hero, empowering us all to take the transformative Tostan program and principles of human rights to poor communities everywhere.

The extraordinary Molly Melching has won dozens of prestigious awards for her humanitarian work and made her dream a reality.

"The future belongs to those who believe in the beauty of their dreams."

Eleanor Roosevelt, the First Lady of the United States from 1933 to 1945, who played a key role in drafting the Universal Declaration of Human Rights.

Chapter 20

Meeting My Soul Sister

I met beautiful, kind, caring, intelligent Millicent Mukindia at the Tostan training in Senegal. A former nurse, midwife and hospital administrator, she is now a health educator in rural villages. A loving wife and mother of three grown-up children and two grandchildren, she is fiercely devoted to her family, her church and serving her community.

Millicent lives in Chogoria, 140 miles north-east of Nairobi, near Mount Kenya National Park, where she runs the vibrant, Faraja Community Centre with her dedicated husband, Pastor Josphat Garama, and their grown-up children, Neema, Eliud and Peter.

Millicent funded building the Faraja centre herself in 2003. Since then, she has been feeding and caring for orphans and vulnerable children and supporting girls and women with vital health education.

When working as an administrator at Chogoria Hospital, Millicent was sponsored to study at University in Scotland. On her return she felt so blessed, she wanted to give back to her community. So, she poured all her savings into the building and called the centre 'Faraja', which means 'comfort' in Swahili, an apt name for this soothing refuge that gives comfort, hope, joy and love to so many.

Millicent explains: "Many families in Chogoria struggle with poverty. Economic instability severely affects individual's capacity to acquire information about their health and sanitation and to make healthy choices.

"We provide health education, outreach medical clinics, agricultural training, and mentoring to families to teach them the knowledge and skills they need to improve their lives.

"Faraja provides basic health education on common illnesses such as malaria and HIV, family planning and hygiene through Mobile Health Clinics in more than 90 villages on the outskirts of Tharaka-Nitha, near Meru.

"We also provide food, clothing, school support and opportunities for play to orphans and vulnerable children."

Many children in the region are orphans or live in vulnerable, unstable families. The Faraja Community Centre provides nutritious meals, clothing and school materials.

Millicent says: "The school materials are especially important for HIV Positive children to reduce the stigma and help them stay in school. We also offer a day care facility for children under five.

A Centre of Comfort and Hope

The Centre has a spacious hall for children to play, with eight rooms, chairs and tables, books and toys and balls. There are also sewing machines for the women to gain sewing skills.

Millicent also teaches health to adolescent girls and supplies reusable menstrual pads through the US charity, *For the Good Period* (4TGP).

Humanitarian worker, Kayce Anderson from Colorado founded the non-profit organisation, with the support of Molly Secor-Turner and Sharon Secor, nursing educators from

North Dakato, and adventurous travel photographer and writer, Kate Lapides.

These dynamic women raise funds to bring reproductive health education and sustainable, re-usable menstrual hygiene pads to girls in rural Kenya.

The 4TGP team makes regular visits to rural Kenya and, with Millicent providing education sessions in the local language of Swahili, they distributed pads to thousands of girls. Millicent is already working hard to support her communities. But she wants to do more.

In fact Millicent and I, although we look as different as chalk and cheese, share a passion. We would love to introduce the *Tostan Community Empowerment Program* (CEP) into remote rural villages and empower women, men and children with knowledge about health and human rights.

We have a vision of bringing the grassroots program to 10 to 20 villages, where knowledge of basis health care is lacking, and lack of knowledge is at the core of sickness and despair.

In West Africa, we witnessed how knowledge about health, human rights, child development, conflict resolution and good governance, conveyed in their own traditional languages, has empowered millions of people living in rural villages.

The Tostan approach requires teams of local people to be trained as facilitators in the Tostan's CEP and teach the program over three years.

By the end of the training, Millicent and I became firm friends and soul sisters, united in a grand vision. Our vision to bring empowerment to remote villages throughout Kenya and other East African countries might seem like an impossible dream.

However, when I look at history, I see that all worthwhile achievements started with someone's daring dream.

And when I look at nature, I see that tiny seeds grow into mighty trees.

> "Let me remind all women that we live longer and better lives when we have sisters we love, not necessarily born in our bloodline or of our race."
>
> *Maya Angelou, African-American Writer and Civil Rights Activist, (1928 – 2014)*

Chapter 21

Period Challenges for Girls in Rural Kenya

My first trip to Kenya was in September 2016. I honoured my promise to visit my new soul sister, Millicent, tagging along with experienced American charity workers.

I was unprepared for travelling the rough rural roads to visit remote communities. My lessons in a multitude of hardships jolted me out of my comfort zone.

I didn't realise how important sanitary pads are for girls and women in Africa. Pads and tampons are essential items widely available to women in the developed world and yet here in the poorer parts of Africa, a lack of pads during menstruation is a source of embarrassment, shame, distress and trauma.

In the backstreets of Nairobi, Christine, at 44, recalls the first time she got her period. "I saw all this blood on my dress at school and when I got home and told my stepmother, she sent me to bed. When my father came home, she told him I'd been raped. From that day on my father looked down on me and treated me badly.

"When I got my period every month, I didn't know what to do about the blood so I tried putting leaves in my panties to soak it up, then I tried dirt and then I tried my father's socks but nothing worked. So, I would go to the maize fields and just sit there for days on my own. I was lonely and sad about missing school because I wanted to get an education."

Eventually, the monthly embarrassment and disruption forced Christine to leave school and give up her dream of becoming a lawyer. However, when she married, a talented seamstress mentored her in the art of sewing.

Now Christine runs a dressmaking business from a cheerful little room festooned with colourful fabric, next to her comfortable home. A team of sewing ladies use two manual Singer sewing machines to produce beautiful dresses, skirts, pants, purses and embroidery. Sheila is one of Christine's star workers.

Sheila is 21 and when she first got her period at 13, she couldn't tell her parents so she told her boyfriend who said he would 'help' her. He gave her money to buy disposable pads in exchange for sex. This is how she survived every month.

The two women are passionate about their charity project called *Days for Girls*, producing hundreds of re-usable cloth sanitary napkins for schoolgirls throughout Kenya.

The ingenious invention comprises a fabric shield, which clicks into panties and holds a panel of absorbent fleece, which can be removed and washed and reused. The shield and pads, panties and soap are put into a pretty fabric drawstring bag.

This snazzy kit empowers a girl to manage her period each month, hygienically and privately with dignity. Most importantly, it allows her to attend school without embarrassment and ensures her education is not disrupted every month.

Christine visits schools far and wide giving talks about managing menstruation and supplying these lovely kits to adolescent girls, which transforms their lives and self-esteem.

Hardy American Helpers

I have joined a road trip with four warm, friendly American women who run a charity called *4 The Good Period*, producing and supplying thousands of reusable cloth pads to girls in remote villages in Kenya.

In our mini-van loaded to the roof with massive bags of supplies, driven by a very patient Mr Livingstone, we have made a stop to visit Christine and learn about this sister charity to explore ways to work together.

Sharon Secur, 66, has been coming to Kenya for over 20 years, as a dedicated humanitarian and fundraiser through the Presbyterian Church in Fargo, Dakota, building strong friendships and partnerships. Sharon and her husband Gary have four daughters and nine grandchildren.

In 1996, she took her daughter Molly on a trip to Kikuyu Hospital in Nairobi when she was a Sophomore in College and undecided about her future career. When Molly witnessed a baby being born, she was awestruck and decided to pursue a career in midwifery and nursing.

Dr Molly Secur-Turner, 40, is now Associate Professor in Nursing and Public Health at North Dakota State University and the mom of three young children.

In 2012, Molly started conducting research and bringing groups of student nurses to rural Kenya. In interviews with schoolgirls and their mothers, she discovered a desperate lack of sanitary products, which was causing girls to miss school. She started bringing supplies of reusable pads.

Molly and Sharon founded the charity 4TGP in 2014. The dynamic duo was joined by Kayce Anderson, 39, a doctor of ecology, and her running buddy, Kate Lapides, 52, a photojournalist from Colorado, who share the passion for empowering girls in Kenya.

Kayce had a friend, Sadler Merle, who manufactures eco-friendly cloth nappies and enlisted him to produce the sanitary napkins, made from non-absorbent fabric for the shield, fitted with soft velvet washable pads.

We are crammed in the heavily laden van, chatting all the way from Nairobi along the impressive Meru Highway, Sharon and Molly, Kayce and Kate and me and Njoki, a stunningly beautiful young Kenyan woman who is returning for a visit home after studying and working in the States for 10 years.

Njoki Kinyua, 30, has just started her new position as Assistant Professor in Environmental Engineering at the University of California in Davis, near San Francisco. She is planning to research the possibility of a bio-gas latrines project.

We set out just after 8am and it is 4pm by the time we reach the lush hilly countryside of the Tharaka-Nithi county where the fertile rust-red soil nurtures flourishing banana, coffee and tea plantations nestled in the foothills of Mount Kenya.

After the long journey, I'm exhausted and ready for a cup of tea when we arrive at the comfortable Chogoria guesthouse, run by the nearby hospital, but my robust travelling companions, despite jetlag, suggest a 'walk'.

I imagine a gentle stroll around the garden, however we head for the bustling marketplace, weaving through rows of roadside stalls bursting with assorted household goods and fresh produce and weary smiling shopkeepers; dodging vehicles and motor bikes, the air filled with traffic noise, bird song and African music.

A Joyful Reunion

Trudging along rocky backroads, chatting with Sharon, I am annoyed with myself for forgetting my water bottle and sunglasses, when suddenly we hear a faint whistle and turn to see beautiful Millicent, who has come to greet us.

This is not how I imagined our reunion, on a dusty track, Millicent in her lovely dress with her beautifully curled hair and radiant smile, and me sweaty, dishevelled and parched! However, it didn't detract from the joy of seeing each other again after meeting in Senegal at the Tostan training course just two months earlier.

"Ah my friend! My sister!" We hug and squeeze each other. Sharon and Millicent have been close friends for 21 years so their reunion overflows with love, and tears and laughter. All the women greet Millicent with that special heartfelt connection that spans countries and cultures.

We walk on for what seems like miles, talking excitedly, until Millicent leaves us to head home, and we return to the guesthouse to a meal prepared by the devoted kitchen staff and clever cooks, Douglas, Anne and Lucy.

After dinner I'm on the point of collapse, when the girls unpack the massive bags full of hundreds of pads and start folding and bagging them. My brain has turned to mush and I'm fumbling hopelessly with the fabric squares, so I excuse myself to crash in my warm double bed, promising to do my share of the huge task tomorrow when I'm fresh!

Spontaneous Sorting

The dynamic women are off early to a Board Meeting, so I am left to contemplate and write and then sit down in the living room to tackle the task. I clear the coffee table and set up a systematic production line, first folding the shields, then the brown velvet fabric into bundles, placing them into zip lock bags and finally into pretty drawstring bags.

I've loved colourful fabric since my fervent teenage attempts at sewing my own clothes, so I am thoroughly enjoying handling the beautiful little bags, which have been lovingly made by countless volunteers, including quilting ladies, in Sharon and Molly's hometown in Dakota. They introduced the novel idea of setting up sewing machines in a local brewery and having fun 'Pints & Pads' nights! Even the men joined in sewing the bags while enjoying a beer!

Engrossed in the pleasant task, suddenly there's a gentle knock at the door and young Silas appears in search of Sharon. He's travelled on the bus to see Sharon, who is sponsoring him at Poly Tech school. I offer him a cup of tea and biscuits and chocolate, and we chat about how he's in final year of Carpentry. His face lights up when he shares his dream of opening his own furniture business.

I ask Silas to help me assemble the packs and we sit together absorbed in the manual work while he tells me about his large family of six siblings. As the eldest boy he is responsible for caring for the young ones and helping with the cows, goats, chickens, and vegetable garden. At 21, he has a girlfriend, who is training in Hairdressing, and they are planning their future together.

Visiting Faraja

It's late afternoon when the women return and we all pile in the car, me with my huge bag full of African storybooks, colouring books, and packets of pencils for the children at Faraja, which means 'comfort' in Swahili. This is a sublime moment, seeing the centre that Millicent, and her husband Josphat, a respected Pastor known by his surname, Garama, have funded and built themselves.

Vulnerable children from resource-poor families, many orphaned, some living with HIV, have come to play and have fun in this cheerful centre and eat a nutritious meal every Saturday since 2003.

Millicent and Garama and their daughter and two sons together with Justus, a retired teacher and other dedicated community members are devoted to caring for the children and making a difference in their young lives. Their loving support has produced many success stories of poor children who have grown up to stay in school and get good jobs.

We are all delighted by Millicent's generous hospitality of afternoon tea and traditional pastries as we sit chatting together in the centre before seeing the sewing room where this multi-skilled lady is starting to produce soft fabric bags and clothes to raise funds for the centre. I have brought a stack of flamboyant fabrics from Senegal and special gold tailor's scissors to support the fledgling social enterprise.

That night, Sharon shares some heart-wrenching stories about the impoverished families she has supported over the years and how she has seen children's hopeless futures transformed by sponsorship that kept them in school to gain qualifications and jobs.

Molly shares the results of her academic evaluations showing how sanitary pads ensure rural girls stay in school. We are all brimming with the creative possibilities of empowering women, men and children, through cross-cultural projects!

In their book, Life-Changing Cross-Cultural Friendships, authors, Gary Chapman and Clarence Shuler write: "Without deep cross-cultural friendships, we will never understand each other. Cross-cultural friendships become life-changing when we learn from each other in mutually beneficial ways."

Chapter 22

The Harsh Realities of Rural Life

After my pleasurable day handling pretty fabrics and socialising, the next day brings a rude awakening. We set off in a four-wheel vehicle driven by our experienced rough road driver, Gbae, into the arid rural area. The dusty red roads are studded with rocks and we bounce along. The dry air is getting hotter as we pass thirsty, desolate fields, where sparse crops are desperate for rain.

We reach the first school, Kajiampau Primary, where the diligent students have created neat rock borders around spindly shrubs and planted thousands of gangly samplings, which will be wonderful when they grow into towering, shady trees.

The Principal is proud to introduce us to each classroom of children, immaculate in their green, blue and gold uniforms. The students are intrigued by their visitors from the US and UK and especially inspired by Njoki, a Kenyan girl who is now very successful, after studying hard and gaining a scholarship.

We leave Kate and her camera and Kayce and her notepad to interview and photograph the girls who received the pad kits in April, to follow up the effects of menstrual hygiene on their school attendance.

This model rural school of 200 students is well established compared to the next isolated school, which has only been going for a few years through support of the Presbyterian churches in the district and their sister churches in the US.

As we pull up next to the mud brick and tin roofed latrines, my head is spinning with the sweltering heat. Principal Benson greets us, with a beaming smile and unbridled enthusiasm for the progress the school is making. He shows us the dank, mud brick, dirt floor classrooms, his cheery office and the staff room, which doubles as a storeroom for sacks of millet.

I'm swept up by Benson's optimism as he demonstrates an English lesson on a wonky blackboard about the difference between 'two', 'too' and 'to' with the sentence: "The boy was too sick to eat two bananas!" We laugh at our cleverness then the impact of the sad sentence hits me.

The Delight of New Classrooms

He proudly shows us the new classrooms under construction, being built from concrete bricks and concrete floor, which will be rendered in plaster; a design similar to the new houses of my former hometown on the Sunshine Coast, Australia. Our group is impressed by the vision of the future for this humble school and Sharon is deeply touched by the good work underway through the funding of her church.

Suddenly, we walk behind the buildings to discover all the school children assembled under a gigantic tree, sitting quietly at their desks, waiting for the visitors to arrive. With a shortage of seating, the children had carried their desks outside.

Community members, teachers, mothers, pupils and guests all participate in this important meeting. Some of the children give a rousing musical performance.

When the children are dismissed, Njoki talks to the adults about the possibility of bringing eco-friendly bio-gas latrines to the school and everyone is curious about how recycling waste into energy would work.

I return to the car to scoff a boiled egg and bread and swig some water. I'm fading fast; drowsy with the heat, hungry, thirsty, tired, busting to pee, and so wimp out on hiking with the children to collect water from the river. I thought I was a hardy traveller but now I'm starting to doubt if I have the stamina for this tough fieldwork.

I'm feeling like a weakling dependent on creature comforts, my cups of tea and my sitting-down, indoor 'work' at my laptop.

We visit a Poly Tech College, where adolescents learn trades such as carpentry, mechanics, computing, tailoring and hairdressing. The teachers are proud of their simple buildings and basic equipment and the success of their students.

I am filled with respect for their determination and achievements in these harsh rural conditions, compared to the luxuries we enjoy in the UK.

The bone-crunching drive home along the rocky roads feels like hours and I am exhausted and mentally and physically shaken up to the point of incoherence and tears when I fall into bed, tormented by a sense of inadequacy and self-doubt, wondering if I could ever handle working in remote communities of such desperate deprivation and poverty.

The world is not fair, I cry to myself.

B&B Comforts

Sleep has restored my sanity and confidence. I am ready to face another day. I am travelling back to Nairobi, to my comfortable room in the delightful Khweza B&B. It's a four-hour pleasant drive through the fascinating countryside, sitting up the back of a jaunty 12-seater van, lost in reverie, enjoying the African gospel songs.

Back at Khweza, the staff are so sweet and kind; Carol and Daniel on the front desk, Wilson and Zedekiah on hospitality, Mary, who cleans the bathrooms beautifully, Abigail, the chef, and Grace and Victor serving meals at the rooftop restaurant that overlooks miles of high-rise buildings, workmen hammering, precariously balanced on planks, amid splashes of purple jacaranda.

The friendly staff makes me feel at home and handsome young Wilson with his dazzling smile is teaching me Swahili.

But that's another story.

"My life belongs to the community, and as long as I live, it is my privilege to do for it whatever I can. I want to be thoroughly used up when I die, for the harder I work, the more I live. Life is no 'brief candle' to me. It is a splendid torch which I have got hold of for a moment, and I want to make it burn as brightly as possible before handing it on to future generations."

George Bernard Shaw, Irish Playwright and Political Activist (1856 – 1950)

Chapter 23

Meeting Beautiful Eyael

After my trip upcountry to Chogoria I joined a spectacular safari trip with Absolute Africa and travelled through the Maasai Mara, Tanzania, Rwanda and southern Uganda. You can read all about these intrepid adventures in my book, Africa Matters. Before I left East Africa, I took a quick trip to Ethiopia for a very special reason.

I have flown from Nairobi to Addis Ababa to meet Eyael, a little girl I've sponsored through *Compassion* for 12 years since she was eight. I started the sponsorship in Australia in 2004 and continued with the monthly payments when we moved to the UK in 2009.

Now in 2016, Eyael is a young woman of 20 who has travelled with a project worker over 300 kilometres on a public bus for seven hours from her rural home in Yirgalem in the southern region where she lives with her parents and three brothers and three sisters.

This is an exciting and emotional day! I'm in the Ag Place Hotel, a pleasant Three Star hotel, waiting for Eyael to arrive with her project worker, the Visit Host and a driver, who will take us around for the day.

When I explain why I'm here, Ganet, the charming hotel manager, invites us to sit in the private VIP lounge.

When Eyael walks in the foyer I am blown away. She is a stunningly beautiful young woman with sparkly brown eyes, a dazzling, shy smile, wavy black hair, honey complexion and the elegant poise of a model! My eyes fill with tears. I am choked up and filled with joy and pride. We hug and look deeply into each other's eyes with a connection that goes right to the heart.

The Visit Host, Meheretab, speaks impeccable English and the national Ethiopian language of Amharic. He translates between the two of us. I ask Eyael and the project worker, Birhane, about their journey the previous day and they say all was fine, despite a much-publicised, government-declared State of Emergency.

I ask if she has visited Addis before and she says only when she was a toddler, so coming to the city is a big event she has been excited about for weeks.

I discover she is soon to complete high school, where she has excelled as an outstanding student, and will then do two years of preparatory school before applying to University. When I ask what career she wants to follow, I almost fall off the chair when she says: "Journalism. I have been inspired by you to be a journalist!" I am deeply touched. I can't believe that I've had such an impact on this young girl just by donating money every month.

Bonding Across Cultures

Through Meheretab, she tells me she has an ambition to be a television presenter and I say that with her beauty and intelligence she is sure to succeed. I tell her my own beautiful daughter Justine is an award-winning filmmaker in London with her boyfriend Andy, who is also a drummer in a rock band. She is very interested and wants to know all about my family.

I say that when I started sponsoring her in 2004, we lived on the Sunshine Coast in Australia and how we moved to the UK seven years ago, how my son Daniel is an entrepreneur and is married with a little son, how my husband Andrew is a business coach and trainer. She wants to know if we all still live together and I explain that my children are grown up and live in London and how we live in the country, an hour by train outside the city, with our cocker spaniels and hens. I show her photos of the whole family.

Eyael tells me about her family. Her parents farm their land and grow avocados, papaya, spices and coffee. I say how I adore avocados! Her eldest sister is a midwife, and her brothers are studying engineering at university while her little sisters are still at school.

We are building a strong bond as we get to know each other. I suggest we go clothes shopping, the universal, cross-cultural activity that all women love! We hit the mall with Meheretab valiantly trying not to get bored as us girls work through the racks. Eyael tries on several outfits and settles on a long olive-green dress and a stylish fitted skirt with a burgundy top. This girl's got taste! I agree to buy all three items and she is delighted and plans to share the new outfits with her sisters.

Our driver, Solomon, takes us to a shady tropical outdoor restaurant attached to the National Museum and I get an education about Ethiopian cuisine! We all have Ingera bread made from fermented teff flour with a holey texture that looks like coral.

We break off pieces and squash them in our fingers to scoop up the delicious spicy stews. Meheretab explains that Ingera is a healthy staple made in every home and eaten twice a day.

Life-Changing

Over our meal, Meheretab shares that he was also a sponsored child from the age of seven. He has never met his American sponsors however he is deeply grateful for the financial support that changed his life. He has just completed his second degree in Public Policy and works as a Counsellor and lay Pastor ministering to the needy.

He says: "Education has developed in me a good heart with a desire to do good for others. I have a strong belief in God and believe that every sponsored child has a God-given purpose. I do this hosting work to give back to Compassion because of the difference it made to me and all it does for so many children."

I ask Eyael what sponsorship has meant for her. She says: "If I was not in the Compassion program going to school would not be easy. My brothers and sisters did not get this privilege. All my needs are being provided for from the money you send. My parents have a big family. They could not afford the school registration, uniforms and books. And the money helps my whole family. It buys soap and cooking oil and grain."

I am flabbergasted. I did not realise my sponsorship over 12 years has meant so much to this precious girl and her family.

Meheretab says there are 400 Compassion projects throughout Ethiopia. Each project supports 250 children with just four hard-working staff; a Project Director, Accountant, Health Worker and Social Worker. They do an incredible job caring for so many youngsters, getting them through school and doing regular health checks and family support.

The next stop is Addis Ababa University, which was formerly the Emperor's Palace. We stroll through the beautiful gardens in the gentle sunshine and Meheretab says the flourishing, government-funded university has several campuses and student accommodation. Around 60,000 students come from all over the country to learn from the best academics in Ethiopia. This is where he studied and got his qualifications and direction in life.

I immediately have a vision of Eyael attending this university doing media studies and I watch her face light up as she explores the vast academic panorama. I imagine the opportunities this outstanding university would open to her.

Mehertab is an expert on Ethiopian history and culture and shows us around the university museum, eloquently explaining the intricacies of the country's rich cultural heritage and ancient sacred sites. He says Ethiopian is a peace-loving country with a population of over 90 million and 80 nationalities speaking 80 different languages and following the two main religions of Christianity and Islam, all co-existing in harmony throughout nine distinct regions.

Next we visit the National Museum where I meet Lucy, the renowned fossil that dates back three million years, which was discovered in Ethiopia by archaeologists in 1974. We stroll around the museum looking at artefacts and paintings and opulent relics from the Emperors' era. Eyael is fascinated and loves the history and culture of her country and wants to share it with the world.

When we say our goodbyes back at my hotel, there are tears and hugs, greetings to each other's family and my heartfelt promise that I will continue to support her through university and into her television career.

Meeting my beautiful girl has been profound. My heart is overflowing with love and respect for Eyael and her family. And I'm imagining her wonderful future.

"I want to build a community where women of all races can communicate and ... continue to support and take care of each other. I want to give women a space to feel their own strength and tell their stories. That is power."

Beyonce, American Singer, Songwriter, Record Producer, Dancer, and Actress. She is regarded as one of the most successful performers of her generation.

Chapter 24

Dreaming the Same Dream

My second trip to Kenya was one year later in September 2017. On my first trip, I dipped my big toe in community work, this time I was willing to dive in.

Squashed in with 12 other passengers, with one whole seat dedicated to my pile of luggage, I am travelling by matatu from Nairobi on a four-hour drive upcountry through lush green tropical vegetation and rusty-red soil fields, gazing out the window at bustling roadside stalls.

Soaking up the sun and breeze, I sit munching potato crisps and crunchy peanuts, next to pretty Evelyn, a teenager clutching her backpack. Then after two hours of companionable silence, she whispers: "I have only one parent now." She is returning to her village for her father's funeral. A knot of sorrow tightens in my chest: "I'm sorry," I say softly. My words are so inadequate.

Millicent, beaming and beautiful, and her strong and kind husband, Pastor Garama, welcome me with an afternoon meal in the Faraja Community Centre, a sturdy building of painted brickwork.

The colourful room with animal murals, where the boisterous children play, laugh, dance and sing, is a vast uncluttered space. However, the empty room has no basic amenities - no plumbing, no electricity, no kitchen to cook the children food!

The ladies make dishes of rice and beans at home and transport the food to the centre.

I meet Fridah, who is employed in the sewing room making impressive African fabric bags, and Faith and Robert, who Millicent is mentoring and training as Facilitators to take health and human rights education into the remote villages.

I am happy to be here in this blessed place that I've been visualising day and night – while drifting off to sleep, waking up, under the shower, driving along country lanes and on the slow train to London - since my last visit exactly one year ago.

Settling into the Guesthouse

I'm staying in a ramshackle guesthouse built of faded grey tin sheets and timber by a British doctor in the 1920s in the tranquil compound attached to the busy hospital. The intriguing old house has several dormitory-style bedrooms and three other guests have left to hike Mount Kenya. I have the spacious house all to myself. My small room has a single bed, cheerful blue floral duvet and rock-hard pillow. I find an old soft pillow stashed in a cupboard and save my neck from cramps!

Mastering the squat toilet is an interesting exercise so I opt for the flushing toilet. My shower is scorching hot. The other shower is freezing cold… nothing in between! I discover how to adjust the temperature after a few days, just in time to wash my hair!

Millicent introduces me to her American friends, Beth and Larry and Martha and Jim, Doctors and Community Workers who live in the hospital houses nearby. They are kind, caring people dedicated to sharing their skills with the locals.

I take my breakfast and dinner, lovingly prepared by smiling Douglas and Anne, in the other comfortable guesthouse where I stayed last visit, just a short walk across the garden.

Jane, the gardener, has the entrepreneurial finesse to multi-skill and put down her rake and sell me a bag of scones!

I dine with Josh, an enthusiastic young American Doctor volunteering at the hospital, Mark, a Kenyan Surgeon who can work up to 16 hours straight to finish a complicated operation, and Kerre, a visiting Dentist, doing his monthly clinic at the hospital, when patients from all over the district come for urgent dental treatment.

Our Shared Vision

The next day, Millicent and I sit together and share our vision for the Faraja Community Centre. Mystically, I have been dreaming of installing a much-needed kitchen and so has she!

In some inexplicable cosmic intersection of dreams, we have been dreaming the same dream - me in secret journals in my secluded home in rural England, and Millicent in prayers in her church in rural Kenya!

As we sip coffee, we dream together of cooking classes for young and old, making nutritious food for all, planting a community vegetable garden and keeping hens to provide fresh eggs. We imagine expanding the sewing project into making reusable shopping bags and mending donated clothes for ladies to sell in the markets.

We dream up the possibility of bringing volunteers to the centre from the UK, Europe, US, Australia and other countries to share our cultures in a multitude of enriching ways in a grand 'voluntourism' venture, combining community work with exhilarating safaris!

We laugh and cry and smile until our cheeks ache! Now the dream is spoken out loud we both know we have made a commitment and a promise to the children, the community, in fact, the whole of Kenya and those people who want an exciting opportunity to Make a Difference.

An Attack of Doubt

Later in the afternoon, I am alone and overwhelmed with anxiety. Suddenly imaginary cynical voices are taunting me: 'Just how are you going to make it all happen?' I'm tormented by details, doubts and questions and oppressed by grey clouds of pessimism.

My mind is spinning when I join Mark and Kerre for dinner. We share our philosophies about the crushing unfairness of poverty. We lighten the mood with entertaining stories, laugh and joke and connect across cultures through our shared concern for suffering humanity.

When I return to my little room, my confidence has returned because our warm conversation has reminded me why I am here and why I am doing this: for the love of these people.

Giving Birth

The heavy rain pounds the tin roof all night, but I feel safe and snug and wake up with the realisation that this ambitious project is like having a baby. After gestation, a mother gives birth and the overwhelmed new parents do not have a clue how they are going to raise this baby over the coming years. They don't know exactly how they will solve the countless problems and challenges ahead. The nervous yet determined parents only know they must take care of their precious child day by day. And so they step bravely into the unknown journey!

Years ago, when I gave birth to my beautiful daughter, I launched my newspaper column, *Family Matters*, writing that: 'Giving birth is the ultimate act of faith'.

The time to 'give birth' has come again at a more mature stage of life. My Kenyan soul sister, Millicent and I are committed to raising Baby Faraja into an inspirational, dynamic force for good. And together, without knowing exactly how, we are embracing an ultimate act of faith.

"Birth isn't something we suffer, but something we actively do and exult in."

Sheila Kitzinger, British Natural Childbirth Activist and prolific Author on childbirth and pregnancy. (1929 -2015)

Chapter 25

Giving and Receiving, Loving and Laughing

Pulling stuff out of my battered duffel bag, it's only September 2017, but it feels like Christmas! I felt pure joy in giving the gifts I've been collecting for months while Millicent and her team express pure delight in receiving loads of goodies for Faraja.

My bag is crammed full of good quality, second-hand colourful clothes I'd bought from charity shops back home in Tenterden, Kent to donate to the local ladies to sell in the markets and make income for themselves with a percentage going to Faraja.

I give Fridah sewing supplies I'd bought on Amazon, give Millicent musical instruments, games and books for the children and Faith and Robert notebooks, pens and stationery for their fieldwork taking health information to remote villages; items I'd bought from Poundland that can make their work easier.

I ask Fridah to hem a dress and long skirt and take in some baggy pants for me as part of the mending project, which generates income for Faraja. Caring visitors from other countries can bring clothes to support this little income-generating business and other useful resources to support the work of the centre.

Planning the Renovations

And then I show Millicent and Garama my idea for the kitchen in the corner of the large, spacious room, for use in the feeding program for the kids and how we can teach nutritious cooking classes and even have a café that draws in the whole community. We discuss how we could install flush toilets and go outside to the rough but fertile ground and visualise a community vegetable garden.

The dynamic and dedicated couple are overwhelmed with excitement, saying they have always wanted to make these improvements to the centre but lacked the funds.

So now the vision for adding the electricity and plumbing and kitchen and expanding the services of Faraja will be possible with some enthusiastic volunteers pitching in with the labour and a fundraising campaign amongst supporters in the UK, Australia and the States. A realistic plan is starting to form in our minds and hearts, which already feels unstoppable and achievable.

The Friday night party at the guesthouse for the hospital staff and their gorgeous children is a fun-filled occasion with a potluck dinner and rowdy games and quizzes.

My instant new friends warmly welcome me to join in.

Meeting The Faraja Kids

Saturday is my first experience meeting the Faraja kids. It's such a pleasure to watch the children sitting quietly and tucking into their hearty meal of rice and beans before playtime erupts, with boys kicking balls and doing handstands and filling the room with laughter.

Around 30 children, aged 4 to 14, come to the centre every Saturday for food and fun! They are vulnerable children from troubled, unstable families and many are orphans living with relatives in poor conditions.

I introduce myself as 'Mama Dee' and then ask each child to come forward and write their name and age in my book. It is such a simple exercise, but the children are enthralled watching intently and applauding riotously as each child completes the task and beams with pride!

But my idea for singing and dancing is a bit of a flop! I'd brought a Jawbone speaker to sync to my iphone playlist, but the music isn't loud enough above the noise of the excited kids. I decide to buy an old-fashioned CD player for next week's session and Millicent suggests we teach the children the words to the songs before they try to sing them! What a good idea! In my enthusiasm to jump in, I have overlooked the obvious!

But Pastor Garama saves the day by telling the kids an animated Bible story about the Good Samaritan with the message of being kind and helping each other.

Dinner with new American Friends

Beth and Larry from Alaska are living in a house in the hospital compound. Larry is a Senior Doctor training medical staff and Beth is a Human Rights Lawyer. They are dedicated humanitarians and Christians devoted to Making A Difference to the community here during their two-year tenure.

They kindly invite Millicent and Garama and me for dinner on Saturday night and over a delicious meal of spaghetti we talk about the volatile politics of Kenya with a second disruptive election being called and we all agree that peace is the most important issue for people struggling each day with poverty.

Ree'L and Jason, a Paediatrician, and their young son Silas pop by. The adventurous family from Los Angeles are devoting five years to working here. Ree'L is a Business Expert and has volunteered to create a new website for Faraja and so I offer to write the content. It is funny how things just flow naturally with like-minded people coming together!

Sunday is for Praise and Worship

I wake up at 5am to the beautiful sound of the girls at Boarding School singing hymns in rich harmonies that float across the tranquil gardens. Sunday is devoted to church, and I see groups of men and ladies dressed in immaculate suits hurrying off to services at an assortment of churches throughout the vibrant community.

I join the congregation of Pastor Garama's Baptist Church to sing hymns together, and hear his inspiring sermon, in English, Meru and Swahili. It is a wonderful, uplifting experience worshipping God and praying together.

Making New International and Local Friends

That night in the guesthouse, over dinner, young Uli, a student from Germany, and young Mark, a Kenyan Surgeon, and myself talk about the challenges of social change and how the beauty of God's own country gets into your soul. Looking at a faded map on the wall of East Kenya, Mark points out some of the most glorious locations to visit, which I add to my wish list!

The idea of bringing groups of visitors to volunteer in the Faraja centre combined with experiencing adventurous wildlife safaris is taking shape in my mind.

So on Monday morning, drenched in sunshine, Millicent and her friend Rebecca, driven in the van by her son Eliud, collect Beth and me to visit the imposing hotel being built nearby.

From the outside, the Snow Peak Hotel, on the busy main road, looks like a building site with the top floor still under construction but inside the lower area is impressive with shiny marble floors, 14 pristine guest rooms, a busy restaurant overlooking the rainforest, stylish bar, and spacious conference room.

Kuka, the owners' daughter, is a vivacious woman with an irresistible sense of humour. She shows us around and we all agree that Snow Peak would provide quality accommodation at a very reasonable rate for groups of visitors. I didn't realise at the time that Kuka would become a cherished friend.

With Beth and Rebecca opting to walk back to the hospital, Eliud drives Millicent and me to check out another accommodation option. Driving through lush farmlands we reach the idyllic Kilimo Talii resort with nine beautiful thatched-roof huts providing luxurious privacy to guests amid the tranquil tropical garden.

Relaxing with soft drinks in the traditional circular restaurant, Eliud tells me he has a German Shepherd puppy called Daisy. As a dog lover missing my two Cocker Spaniels, I'm captivated, and we chat about puppies. I can't wait to meet her!

That afternoon, I get stuck into writing content for the Faraja website, my creativity flowing with enthusiasm. Back home in Kent, my ideas for making a difference were all theoretical but now, being here, the whimsical dreams are in fact feasible!

Tuesday morning, I ceremoniously wave farewell to the three German hikers who have conquered majestic Mount Kenya. Karl, Holger and his son Uli are off for their next adventure in Tsavo National Park to see the awe-inspiring African wildlife: elephants, rhinos, lions, leopards, zebras, giraffes and antelope.

New Colleagues

Meeting with Ree'L over coffee we discuss our shared goal to attract international interest in the humble community centre with its massive potential to transform lives. That afternoon Millicent introduces me to charming David and Justus, retired teachers, who serve on the executive board of the Faraja Community Centre.

When I lay out the vision to install power and plumbing and a kitchen, the men are elated and bursting with ideas. Justus wants to introduce local kids and adults to the wonders of healthy fresh juices made by a Juicer!

I meet Jane, over dinner, who is staying at the main guesthouse while she leads a series of seminars on Preparing for Retirement for hospital staff. I meet her son Paul, a super intelligent young man, highly qualified in maths, science and computer programming, who has driven his mum from Nairobi.

It's Wednesday already and after another morning of working solidly writing the website copy, I venture to the nearby markets with my purse and camera, returning with some delightful photos of colourful street life, a new long dress, a t-shirt, African fabric for Fridah to make bags and bunches of spinach and avocadoes for Douglas and Anne!

Feels Like Home

In less than two weeks I have settled into the funny old guesthouse and the relaxed rhythm of life here. I am soaking up the fragrance of tropical flowers on the gentle breeze, basking in the clear blue skies and caressing sunshine The purple Jacaranda, pink Bougainvillea, pretty Hibiscus, orange Poinciana and red Banksia remind me of my homes on the Sunshine Coast, Australia.

I am overjoyed to meet warm and friendly local people who smile and say 'Jambo, karibu'... 'Hello, you are welcome' and good-hearted humanitarian workers who share the dream to make a difference for people living with the horrendous challenges of poverty.

And my courage to take a risk to commit to the ambitious project of fundraising and recruiting volunteers to build amenities in the Faraja Community Centre has taken me by surprise. Suddenly the impossible seems possible ... if I can just inspire enough people to care.

"If there is any kindness I can show, or any good thing I can do to any fellow being, let me do it now, and not deter or neglect it, as I shall not pass this way again."

William Penn, English Writer and Quaker who founded Pennsylvania during the British colonial era (1644 – 1718).

Chapter 26

The Power to Fly

Something wonderful is taking shape – colourful plans to bring groups of visitors from the UK, Europe, Australia, the US and other developed countries on life-changing trips to Kenya for a combination of volunteering and exciting travel.

I first came across the term 'voluntourism' in 2012 when I met an extraordinary man, John Lawler who founded Madventurer – a scheme for students on their gap year - between high school and university - to volunteer in challenging projects in developing countries with the opportunity to Make a Difference while having a grand adventure.

I interviewed this modest high achiever one sunny day near the Tower of London and was inspired by John's story of starting out with a tiny seed of an idea that grew into the mighty tree of a flourishing worldwide charity. A few months later I did an exciting trip to Ghana as possibly the oldest 'gap year' volunteer in history, and discovered the joy of making heartfelt connections with people living in another culture!

And here I am five years later in rural Kenya returning to the theme of 'voluntourism', excited about the possibility of empowerment and transformation for both visitors and local people.

Millicent and I imagine that international visitors can come and volunteer in the Faraja Community Centre and help with the kids' activities, the ladies' sewing project, nutritious cooking classes and planting the community vegetable garden.

Volunteering is certainly NOT about White People flying in as superior, condescending Saviours to tell poor Black People what to do! Oh no, no, no! Volunteering is about an equal, respectful cultural exchange – a sharing of knowledge, creativity and traditions that becomes enriching and expansive for everyone. For example, visitors can share their favourite recipes with local women who will share their traditional dishes.

Sweet Bananas

Here's how respectful, equal friendship works. On Sunday I gave Anne some chocolate to say 'Asante' for her delicious meals – a real treat for Anne, who, unlike me, doesn't get to have much chocolate! Today Anne gave me a perfect bunch of yellow, dainty Lady Finger bananas from her garden – a real treat for me, who relishes good quality, sweet bananas!

I believe people from different cultures can learn from each other. The cultural exchange adds spice and novelty to bland, jaded lives. And we can make interesting new friends across countries, despite how politicians would divide us and build borders and walls to keep people apart, cultivating ignorance, fear and hostility. The truth is we are all human beings, connected as one big global family – mothers and fathers, brothers and sisters, sons and daughters.

And what about adventure? Together with Millicent and Garama and their sons, Peter and Eliud, we are devising a range of exhilarating trips to integrate into a three-week stay in rural Kenya.

On arriving in Nairobi, groups will visit the heart-warming *Giraffe Centre* and *Elephant Orphanage* before heading upcountry where trips will include game drives to see African wildlife in spectacular Meru National Park or safaris on the Maasai Mara, staying in beautiful eco lodges; camping in Mount Kenya National Park, field trips to the remote villages with Millicent, day trips to the nearby tranquil waterfall lagoon, visits to lush hillside coffee and tea plantations and optional extras such as visiting the exotic tribal Maasai people and finally the ultimate add-on for those who are up for experiencing a tropical paradise?

Magnetic Mombasa

When I first saw the word 'Mombasa' on the map of Kenya and neighbouring Diani Beach (with my name on it!), I was enchanted by the musical sound of the word as it rolled around my tongue. I quietly vowed to visit. However, I never made it to the legendary coastal town on my last trip in 2016.

Mombasa is apparently a laid-back hippy haven of non-stop reggae parties and hot and steamy, glorious beaches, full of beautiful bodies basking in endless sunshine.

Over and over the hypnotic word 'Mombasa' keeps cropping up. People whisper about romantic adventures camping under the stars with a view of Mount Kilimanjaro on the way to Mombasa!

And now the long-awaited new train from Nairobi to Mombasa is finally running, taking travellers right through spectacular Tsavo National Park with wild animals roaming free – you can spot buffalo, zebra, giraffes, lions, elephants from the window of the train!

The word 'Mombasa' evokes rapturous reactions. While having lunch – a mountain of masala chips and Spanish omelette - on the balcony overlooking the rainforest at the Snow Peak Hotel, Pastor Garama's face lights up at the mention of Mombasa! Suddenly he is lost in the revelry of fond memories of the magical place where he grew up with three brothers and three sisters, running free!

Young Mark, the surgeon I met at the guesthouse, raves about Mombasa as paradise, and warns that once you succumb to Mombasa's seductive charms, you never want to leave!

For the Wild at Heart Only

For the wild at heart and the eternally youthful, I'm imagining running trips to escape the bleak English winter for adventurous travellers who also want to go MAD and Make A Difference. The question is, can you see yourself joining the life-changing voluntourism movement?

The metamorphosis of the lowly caterpillar into a beautiful butterfly is an inspiring symbol of transformation. But have you imagined what it actually feels like to be that mundane grub, wriggling along munching through leaves mindlessly, running on instinct, never looking beyond the next leaf, until one day you decide to spin yourself a reclusive cocoon where you retreat to contemplate your life's higher purpose. While in this dark slumber something miraculous is taking place. You are being transformed! Suddenly you emerge with shock and exhilaration – you are reborn in a different form – with a set of beautiful wings with the power to fly!

Chapter 27

At Home in the Heartland of Kenya

The vision started to form in hazy outlines during my mind-expanding trips to Chogoria in September 2016 and September 2017. It wasn't until my third trip in February and March of 2018, that concrete plans were laid.

The Project

The grand plan is to install a modern kitchen in the Faraja Community Centre to expand services to the whole community. We share a vision to offer a variety of meals, using the healthy produce grown in this fertile region, to the vulnerable children who converge on the centre every Saturday for a meal of beans and rice, stories, songs and ball games and lavish doses of nurturing from Mama Millicent and Pastor Garama.

This loving husband and wife are passionately devoted to improving the quality of life for families throughout Chogoria, a vibrant market town set in the heart of the lush farmlands of Tharaka-Nithi in the foothills of Mount Kenya.

On my arrival, we brainstorm without limits, imagining teaching cooking and nutrition classes to the local ladies, holding Pizza Nights for the youth, Mums and Babies get-togethers, Movie Nights, Family Events, Men's Fellowship, all sorts of training workshops and so much more.

We are tingling with excitement at the possibilities that a new kitchen will unleash!

I have some guys from a Kitchen Company in Nairobi travel four hours by matatu (public bus) to draw up a design and give us a quote on the project. When I get the email, my heart sinks! The design is impressive but not exactly what we'd asked for and the quote is way too high! I realise the process of communicating clearly and negotiating in the planning stage is going to take much longer than my four-week stay!

Another roundtable meeting with Millicent and Garama and board members and we agree to go 'pole pole' – that's Swahili for 'slowly slowly'. I decide to return next year for a three-month stay to help with installing the kitchen, an extra water tank and filter system and new electrical wiring.

Meantime we tackle the task of repainting the floor and courtyard in the beautiful rust-red colour of the earth. Garama, with son, Peter and young Silas, quickly transform the place in the first stage of the Faraja Community Centre makeover!

The Cast of Characters

I am staying at the delightful Snow Peak, an unlikely name for a hotel surrounded by a leafy tropical garden of towering palm trees, exotic ginger plants and pretty purple bougainvillea, a tinkling stream and sweet singing birds. The locals proudly explain that when you look up you can glimpse the snow-capped peak of majestic Mount Kenya!

You know the feeling when you stay at a hotel so long it feels like a second home? I sure have settled into a pleasant routine of a leisurely breakfast on the tranquil balcony while trying Kenyan dishes and making new friends.

The owners of the newly opened hotel, the lovely Justin and Sylvia Njeru are making me so welcome!

Justin Njeru Ng'entu is also a coffee farmer with a depth of knowledge about the region's history and he regales me with entertaining stories of the colonial past.

Under British rule it was illegal for local farmers to grind and drink their own high-quality coffee, which was seized for export at massive profits for the Brits, while farmers were paid very little.

In an ironical twist, I had bought a packet of Mount Kenyan coffee in Waitrose in the UK and gave it to Justin along with a coffee plunger as a gift. We sit together savouring the aromatic coffee and dreaming up ways he can sell his superb coffee direct to the public!

Garama has also discovered 'London Tea' (in preference to weak milky African-style tea) and is enjoying the ritual of taking strong tea mid-morning and afternoon with biscuits! This is a new vice he can blame on me!

I buy huge avocados for a few shillings in the market and make guacamole with Sylvia and Joy. The avocados in this fertile paradise are so plentiful they fall on the ground to be eaten by happy pigs! Mash them up with salt, garlic, chilli and lemon and serve with African-style chapatti and suddenly the locals are discovering why avocados are so popular in other countries! I love this cross-cultural exchange!

My favourite Kenyan dishes are vegetable samosas, Bhajia, which are deep fried scalloped potatoes with coriander, and Spicy Cowpea Curry.

The young staff – Peter, the chef, Linda and Joy, the pretty waitresses, Kelly, who is in charge of Housekeeping with impeccable high standards, Davis, training in hotel management and Daniel Kiambi, the gardener – are all so friendly and amused by Aussie accent and funny ways!

My African 'Twin Sister'

But when I chat with Kuka, Mr and Mrs Njeru's vivacious daughter, I believe I've met my African 'twin'. We are so alike with our shared backgrounds in media, politics, and psychology, with our secret passions for romantic movies and country music, we hit it off and can't stop talking for hours! Kuka already has a real twin sister, Kuki, so I accept the role of 'imposter twin' and we laugh at how similar we look as 'twins', comparing our chocolate and vanilla skin!

In the restaurant after a huge lunch with Kuka and American friend Ree'L, I am texting, when I look up to see this larger-than-life character sporting an Akubura hat and floral shirt! Micheu Obadiah is a genuine one-off!

He loves to play his guitar and sing, and we immediately burst into old songs; Leonard Cohen, Bob Dylan, Elton John, the Seekers! Who would believe I'd find someone in Kenya who knows every word of *'Another You'*! It's an unusual way to meet someone but life's too short to waste an opportunity to sing! So we sing together in the restaurant and the young ones are now convinced I am quite mad! I'm planning to bring my guitar next time so we can strum and sing around the campfire!

I discover on an impromptu nature walk that Obadiah is an expert on medicinal plants of East Africa and a keen bird watcher, who can mimic the beautiful calls of all the local species!

I meet Larry, a rugged Texan Paramedic, who is doing a vital project setting up emergency services for villages in the remote areas of Kenya. He shares stories of life in the spectacular scorching desert of his home state, adventures in the Mexican wilderness, working in Yellowstone National Park, and setting up medical services in poor countries all over the world.

There's James, a Kenyan man who has returned home after living more than 20 years in the UK. He is now embarking on an innovative farming project with 30 families with his dynamic young wife, Ann and their adorable little girl, Hope. And there's Alpha, a Social Worker who has worked with charities and NGO's all over Africa and has a business idea for growing coconuts in Mombasa.

I've become good friends with the Garama brothers, Peter who is the proud new dad of baby Oliver with his beautiful partner Purity and Eliud who is training in community development work with his mum and her team.

Millicent has become my Kenyan sister. She has so much wisdom and strength and exudes empathy and bubbles with laughter. Pastor Garama is my Kenyan brother, so protective, caring and kind.

Patrick is my jovial driver and tour guide in Nairobi. He makes sure I'm picked up from Kenyatta Airport and safely taken to my accommodation at the comfortable Milele Hotel, run by the PCEA – Presbyterian Church of East Africa - for a night's rest. Then he drives me to the bustling city centre to board a crowded matatu for the scenic journey to Chogoria.

My friend, Edmund Kiprono, whom I met on safari with *Absolute Africa*, now runs his adventure tours throughout Kenya. He's an experienced tour guide with a wealth of knowledge and irrepressible sense of humour.

My friend, Ndabahariye Joseph, whom I met in Kisoro, Uganda runs an amazing tour company called *Birasa Tours* showing visitors the spectacular sights, including the Mgahinga Gorilla National Park. Joseph champions the cause of the impoverished Batwa People. He is a dedicated humanitarian and environmentalist.

I feel loved-up and connected to my network of new friends while strengthening my bond with Facebook friends and followers in this cross-cultural immersion.

A Sense of Belonging

I'm becoming a local. I know this because after a trip to the colourful, bustling markets, laden down with bags of bananas, mangoes and peanut butter and African fabric, I jump on the back of a 'boda-boda' motor bike and whiz along the road, with my blonde hair flying in the breeze and the locals laughing at the 'mzungu' (white person).

One day, we pile in the van with Peter and Purity nursing baby Oliver and Grandma Millicent beaming with pride in the back with Eliud capably behind the wheel and me in the passenger seat gazing out at the spectacular rolling hills as we head for Meru. Only problem is traffic is gridlocked approaching the bustling town and we sit and sweat for over an hour, crawling along inch by inch. But 'hakuna matata' we eventually arrive and have lunch. The meals take over an hour to emerge from the kitchen because all food is prepared from scratch. I'm learning that patience is an essential attribute in laid-back Kenya.

So we hit Tuskys department store and buy a whole lot of baby stuff for little Oliver who sleeps his way through the hot and steamy shopping expedition! And we also buy the paint and rollers and poles for the floor painting job!

On another busy Saturday the boys and I head for Chuka to buy mobile phones. I have succumbed. As an Apple devotee, I cross to the Dark Side and purchase my first Samsung to use exclusively with Safaricom in Kenya. My Goodness, it's complicated setting up a new phone! So thankfully Peter, who is an IT whiz, gets me all sorted and connected to social media and every app ever invented. (I'm exaggerating now!)

And Peter and I are working together to create a Faraja Facebook Page and enrich the Faraja website to build a following of international supporters and encourage visitors to this beautiful region.

I'm starting to get to know the little kids as individuals. The tiny pretty little girls whose big brown eyes and dazzling smiles light up the room and the lanky teenage boys who can kick a soccer ball with incredible force! The children have a little party with bread and crisps and bananas as extras on their beans and rice and then we spend ages playing ball games, colouring with crayons, and having stories and singing Swahili songs.

The rainy season has come early. During the Faraja Kids' Club, a torrential downpour drenches the courtyard within minutes and the thundering noise on the roof is frightening. However, the heavy rain stops quickly, and the brilliant green vegetation sparkles and the air is fresh and fragrant. And no one back at the hotel is worried when the power goes out and we're plunged into darkness! Hakuna matata. I go to bed with my Spotify country music playlists and when I wake up the power is back on.

Perfect Climate

I lived for 20 years in the sub-tropics of south-east Queensland, Australia where the sweltering humidity over summer makes you pour with sweat and the relentless sun gives you a permanent squint and you burn your feet on the scorching sand trying to dash to the ocean for a swim.

I've lived in the UK since 2009 where the bleak winters make you hibernate indoors with a case of SAD (Seasonal Affective Disorder) or risk a frost-bitten nose on a rugged-up walk through the eerie bare trees of the muddy woodlands with your shivering dogs.

Chogoria is close to the equator, near Mount Kenya. The high altitude means the climate is ideal, boasting pure hot days and clear blue skies with cool evenings and cool mornings so you can snuggle up and sleep without raising a sweat!

Like Goldilocks, I've found the perfect middle ground – not too hot, not too cold – just right! 'Asante sana' - Thank you very much!

I've given myself a Kenyan name, 'Diani' after the idyllic beach near Mombasa. This forever-young hippy feels right at home in rural Kenya – a beautiful place with a cast of character and a purposeful project to keep me busy.

"The purpose of life is a life of purpose."

Robert Byrne, American Author

Chapter 27

Njeru's Passion Captured on Film

I was serious now. It was time to move from a vision and a plan to the reality of installing the new kitchen at Faraja. For the first three months of 2019 I stayed at the endearing Snow Peak Hotel while I committed to completing our ambitious project. But first, a creative side project: making a film about the extraordinary Mr Njeru. I enlisted the expertise of enthusiastic young filmmakers, Victor Murithi and Michael Kimotho Omotho and together we told his story.

Mr Justin Njeru has devoted his life to coffee farming in the lush tropics surrounding majestic Mount Kenya.

But the first time he tasted his own quality coffee was when I visited from the UK and stayed at his hotel and gave him a bag of freshly ground beans grown on the slopes of Mount Kenya that I'd bought from a supermarket in London!

Sitting together on the shady balcony of the Snow Peak hotel, he slowly pushes down the coffee plunger and chuckles with glee at the irony!

In 2019, at the age of 76, married his devoted wife, Sylvia for 47 years, father of six high achieving adults and grandfather of 13 youngsters, Mr Njeru has a renewed sense of purpose!

Revenge is Sweet

He is finally defying the British colonialists! And the taste of revenge is sweet!

He explains that in the 1950s the British rulers made it illegal for the local people in the fertile coffee-growing region of Meru to drink their own coffee. Instead, the lucrative product was exported for the burgeoning mass markets in the UK and profits were greedily grabbed by the wealthy elite. Hard-working Kenyan coffee farmers were paid peanuts!

He reflects: "I remember when coffee was first introduced to this area, people, even the growers were not allowed to drink coffee because it was not available in the shops. The only way one could drink coffee was to use crude means like grinding the beans with stones and boiling it. If you were caught you would be prosecuted. You would be taken to the Chief and punished. Our coffee was all being exported. It was for export to Britain, for the white man."

Passion of a Lifetime

Mr Njeru grew up learning every aspect of coffee growing from his father. He has witnessed green berries turn into ruby cherries for countless seasons and he's harvested and processed millions of sacks of beans.

"When coffee was first introduced in 1950 my father planted coffee. We didn't have farm implements so the children would dig the holes and watch as the trees were planted. So I developed an interest in growing coffee as a child. It has been my life-long passion."

He nurtures 15,000 trees spread over 17 acres of idyllic farmland of volcanic red soil, basking under blue skies of endless sunshine and generous rainfall, producing the finest coffee in the world.

A Champion of the Growers

He has championed the rights of hundreds of coffee growers in the region as Chairman of the Mount Kenya Fine Arabica Coffee Growers' Association. And yet, even today, many decades after Independence from British Rule in 1963, farmers are still exploited by the middlemen and paid peanuts for their delectable beans.

"Growing coffee is very difficult and the regulations are stringent, especially during harvesting. You must take only the ripe berries of the finest quality. The coffee grown in Kenya is mostly Arabica which is better in quality because of the aroma and the acidity. And growing Arabica is more demanding, the care is more tender, than growing Robusta coffee. We are proud that Kenyan coffee is renowned as the best in the world."

Justice for Justin

While coffee connoisseurs around the world are insatiable for their daily caffeine fix, the farmers of Kenyan do not receive a fair price for their quality product, their arduous labour and their loving dedication to perfection.

But all that can change. Justice for Justin and his fellow coffee growers is possible if they can by-pass the controlling grip of the Coffee Board and sell directly to independent buyers from other countries.

Talking about his hopes and dreams, he states: "Growers should be allowed to do their own marketing and sell to the willing buyer. We are fighting for the right to sell our coffee freely. Development in this region is all pegged to coffee as a cash crop. Coffee has supported education by building schools and allowing parents to pay school fees. I dream of processing and exporting my own coffee as a finished product, rather than a raw material, at fair price."

As international trade markets relax, there is hope that Kenyan farmers will finally receive a fair price for their quality coffee, their expertise and their labour. And maybe the local people will even get to enjoy a freshly ground brew of this elixir of life.

The quirky little film, Njeru's Passion is available on my YouTube channel. I'm hopeful that Mr Njeru's dream will come true and we will find independent international buyers for his superb coffee.

Chapter 29

Spontaneous Acts of Helping

The knowledge, skillsets, and resources that mature-aged people have acquired in their lives is considered ordinary in developed countries. But when you take the same knowledge, skillsets, and resources into poor countries where people lack the basics, you can make an extraordinary impact for good.

In early 2019 while staying at the Snow Peak Hotel in Chogoria, a bustling township set in lush farming country, I made friends with the local people. All sorts of unscheduled issues just seemed to pop up that demanded my spontaneous help, whether I planned for them or not.

Hot Babies

Mary came into the centre carrying her baby boy, Dexter wrapped up tightly in a woollen shawl and knitted bonnet over several layers of clothing, even though the tropical heat was sweltering. The little boy was sweaty and listless. I didn't have to be a medical expert to see that he was over-heated.

I suggested to Mary that she unwrap him, take off the bonnet and outer layer of clothes and lay him on a rug on the floor to cool down. The baby kicked his bare legs in the air and drank some fresh water and was instantly revived.

I had seen other mothers carrying babies and toddlers wrapped up like this in the marketplace and was puzzled. Then I remembered that Scottish missionaries had moved to Chogoria in the 1920s. I suspect the well-meaning ladies advised local mums to adopt baby care methods from the cold climate of Scotland. And keeping babies wrapped up warm became a custom in Chogoria passed down through the generations without question.

Mary told me that if she dared to uncover her baby, older women would berate her as a bad mother and make her feel ashamed. This is how a social norm based on wrong information is enforced.

I chatted with Mary over a cuppa and she mustered the courage to ask me a question. She said Dexter has white spots on his gums and she was told to take him to the Old Woman with the razor blade so she could cut them out. She wanted to know if I thought this was the right thing to do. Shocked and horrified, I advised her that cutting his gums would cause him great pain, injury and possible infection and that she must always take her child to the Chogoria Hospital for proper medical treatment.

Why do these old women want to cut children with rust razor blades, I fumed to myself, in disbelief. I think that the razor blade is the only tool in her medical kit. She has nothing else to offer. And then I felt sad and angry about poverty.

When I asked my medical friend, Larry, he explained white spots on the gums are caused by dehydration. I realised in that brief encounter with Mary that the Faraja Community Centre needs Mums' Groups that offer accurate information to young mothers, so they are not relying solely on misinformation passed down through the generations.

Avocado Breakthrough

I have always loved avocados. So, I was delighted to discover huge, plump avocadoes growing in abundance in Chogoria. However, the locals didn't know what to do with them and the healthy fruits were often left to rot on the ground or given to the pigs to gobble with glee.

So I decided to teach the locals how to make guacamole. A recipe so simple and basic, mashing the creamy green flesh with salt, garlic, chilli and lemon juice, gave the bland avocados extra zing. The result was miraculous! Mrs Njeru started serving the dip with chapatis to guests in the hotel and the delicious dip was an instant hit! I held little workshops for farmers, and they were amazed by the taste and started serving guacamole with rice and beans. Such a small thing as sharing a recipe made a big difference.

Healing Relationships

Benson had heard I was a counsellor and shyly approached me one day asking if he could discuss a problem. We made a time to chat, and he told me that when he was at college, his girlfriend got pregnant, and he was so shocked he told her he didn't want the baby and suggested an abortion. The young girl was heartbroken and returned home to her family and had the baby.

Now two years later, he had matured and wanted to meet his little son, but his former girlfriend was still hurt and angry and refused all contact. Benson didn't know how to persuade her and was constantly sad and upset, longing to meet his son.

I advised him that he first needed to heal his relationship with his former girlfriend before she would agree to any contact with the little boy. I helped him write a Healing Letter, which contained four essential elements: I'm sorry, forgive me, thank you and I understand. In a healing letter it doesn't matter how many times you write 'I'm sorry for…' and list all the things that hurt the other person, and you can say 'Thank you for…' and list all the things you were grateful for in that relationship. You ask for forgiveness and express understanding and love.

Benson's email opened a dialogue with his former girlfriend who vented her pain and anger in reply. I advised him to just receive the tirade without defending himself. Eventually she softened and they made their peace and she agreed to him seeing his little boy.

I was so honoured and grateful to be able to help these young parents heal their pain and reconcile. It was a blessing that they committed to sharing access of their little boy so he will grow up knowing his father.

Malaria Alert

Julie was a waitress at the Snow Peak Hotel and every morning would serve me breakfast on the balcony surrounded by towering trees and chirpy birds. Her beaming smile and cheerful banter filled me with delight. As we became friends, she shared that she had a son who lived with his grandmother in another village.

One morning Julie seemed troubled and when I enquired, she said her little boy was being naughty and pretending to be sick and didn't want to go to school. She was annoyed that he was misbehaving for his grandmother. But I asked her to describe his symptoms and they sounded like malaria.

Symptoms of malaria include fever and flu-like illness, including shaking chills, headache, muscle aches, and tiredness, nausea, vomiting, and diarrhoea. This common tropical disease is transmitted by mosquitoes and can be easily treated if caught quickly.

I told Julie to jump on a bus to the village and take her son to the doctor immediately. I pressed some money into her hand for the fare and some chocolate for the journey. When she returned later in the week, it turns out the boy did have malaria and was treated in time.

As in the case of Mary, I don't pretend to be medically qualified, but I can Google information and recognise a risk. I just happened to be in the right place at the right time.

Aprons, Curtains, Loans, Motorbikes, Friendship

In installing the new kitchen and renovating the community centre there were so many opportunities for spontaneous acts of helping, like paying Fridah to sew some lovely green aprons. The money she earned paid her daughters' school fees. We asked a local lady, Medrine to make the beautiful new curtains. She had been sick and out of work and was grateful for the job.

Young Silas, who I'd met on my first trip in 2016, jumped at the opportunity to assist Fred, our experienced carpenter, with the kitchen job. Two young local lads, Kevin and Collins, did all the painting. Elius, a highly skilled electrician did a superb job with the wiring. A local plumber, James installed the tank and water system.

Millicent and Cathrine, the dedicated lady who has been cooking for the needy children for years, now has a fancy new kitchen to work in.

Paul, a young chef, had borrowed money from a loan shark and was being crippled with exorbitant repayments. I agreed to give him the money to pay the debt in exchange for helping in the kitchen.

I taught Peter, Eliud and Robert how to make pizza, Mexican tortillas and pasta dishes to launch the Faraja Café for the youth of Chogoria.

Benson pranged his mother's car. I covered the repair costs in exchange for him donating Faraja a reconditioned laptop he bought from his cousin.

I hired talented young filmmakers, Victor and Michael, to make a brilliant little film about Mr Njeru, and his life as a coffee grower, so I could promote his quality coffee to buyers back in the UK.

I visited Kelly and her sweet little daughter and delightful extended family on their farm, meeting her great-great grandmother, and seeing their flourishing tea plantation.

I visited Ann and James and beautiful little Hope on their innovative hilltop farm with stunning views.

We travelled to Meru to meet the extraordinary Dr Karambu Ringera, who runs an orphanage, permaculture farm and training centre empowering young people to live their dreams.

Talented guitarist, Obadiah and I had many fun-filled singalongs at the Snow Peak Hotel. My African sister, Kuka and I talked and laughed for hours about all the things we have in common – journalism, politics, psychology, romantic movies and salsa dancing. (She can actually dance! I just dream about dancing!)

I became friends with Larry Hill, a Texan paramedic who has worked in impoverished communities all over the world and helped people through disasters and tragedies.

He was launching a charity called *Medic Outpost*, training first responders in remote villages. These days his charity is thriving, helping thousands of children and adults in poor communities in Kenya, Mexico and other needy countries.

My time in Chogoria was bursting with random acts of kindness and spontaneous acts of helping that nourished my soul. For anyone who is jaded and feels obsolete, I assure you, your talents and skills, knowledge and friendship will be appreciated in the heartland of Kenya.

My Kenyan friends have also helped me in countless ways. They have taught me about their fascinating culture, their many tribes and languages and knowledge of nature. They have shared their qualities of love and joy, kindness and generosity and strength and wisdom. They have taught me acceptance, patience, and the art of living in the moment on 'Kenyan time'. Support is mutual. We enrich each other by giving and sharing.

"Random acts of kindness are those little sweet and grand lovely things we do for no reason except that, momentarily, the best of our humanity has sprung, exquisitely, into full bloom.

You have set your soul free to give for the sheer, beautiful sake of true giving. In giving freely, purely, for no reason and every reason, you move into another person's landscape… because in your heart, that majestically super-human organ, the castle of love, you have felt the spiritual necessity of acting out your love."

Psychotherapist and Author, Daphne Rose Kingma, in writing to foreward to Random Acts of Kindness.

Chapter 30

How a Kitchen is Transforming a Community

Finally, on my fourth trip to Chogoria in 2019, the kitchen project got underway.

I hired the Streamline Designs kitchen company in Nairobi to make the stylish cabinetry, a local plumber, James to install a chlorinator, filter system and new water tank to provide clean, safe water and local electrician, Elias to bring power and lights. Local painters, Kevin and Collins, did a beautiful makeover, painting the walls and floor, two skilful tilers beautified the kitchen walls, and skilful sewing lady, Medrine, made stunning new curtains for the whole centre.

Supervising the installation of the modern kitchen in the rustic building was the biggest challenge of my life! I was propelled out of my comfort zone into hard physical work, tricky problem solving and daily decision-making over two solid months.

And it was a financial stretch. I donated £7,000 of my own money to install the modern galley kitchen in the empty corner of the Faraja main hall, including a stove and fridge and an assortment of appliances and crockery and tables and chairs, along with renovations throughout the building.

Miraculously, we launched the kitchen with a joyful celebration party on March 22, 2019.

The ladies brought fruit and veggies from their shambas (gardens), and we gathered to prepare delicious food to share, including yummy guacamole!

Kuka led the children in the dancing and singing and the youth and elders mingled together to check out the impressive makeover of Faraja and imagine the possibilities for everyone in the community.

The dazzling new kitchen will be the catalyst for expanding the food choices for the children and teaching kids nutrition and cooking, a Mums and Babies Group, a Women's Health Group, a Men's Health Group and a Youth Social Group serving up pizza and music.

We plan to run a daily café, creating a vibrant meeting place for the whole community and international medical workers and visitors who come to climb Mount Kenya.

The Faraja Kitchen will be self-sustaining, making money from the sale of food to cover running costs, pay workers and fund further improvements to the centre.

And we have many exciting ideas for income-generating small businesses including a Sewing Group making African fabric bags; the Malaria-prevention Soap-making Group and a Coconut initiative to transport coconuts from coastal Mombasa to Chogoria to produce nutritious coconut oil, milk, cream and cheese.

Garama, an agricultural expert, is in charge of the flourishing Faraja Vegetable Garden growing tomatoes, peppers, cucumbers, green beans, spinach, lettuce, cauliflower, broccoli and herbs to supply the kitchen.

In the future, the Faraja Community Centre will provide training for local facilitators in health, human rights and stopping harmful practices such as female genital cutting and child marriage in villages all over Kenya.

We aim to be part of the movement for social change.

All this transformation is flowing from the everyday miracle of a kitchen. My soul sister, Millicent and I have realised our beautiful dream in the heartland of Kenya that started three years ago in Senegal! We proved that anything is possible when caring people join together to make a difference.

See the delightful photos of the Kitchen Launch on my blog, Over 50 And Making a Difference.

Chapter 31

In Millicent's Words

It was an exciting day when I travelled out of Nairobi in a big aircraft headed to Dakar, the capital city of Senegal in 2016. I met Diane Priestley when we both attended the Tostan course in Community-led Development and we became great friends.

During the training, we got chatting and Diane told me that she longed to work in Kenya to address health issues, especially preventing female genital cutting. I told her that I had a building in my hometown, Chogoria dedicated to caring for vulnerable children through providing nutritious meals, reading and play materials, school fees and uniforms.

I shared that I also travelled to remote villages in the Tharaka Nithi County as a health educator, teaching about water borne diseases, sexually transmitted infections and reducing the stigma of HIV and encouraging good parenting skills.

Diane was inspired and made a commitment to support my work in Kenya.

Later that year, Diane visited our project, the Faraja Community Centre. She was touched by the inadequacy of the facilities we were using for cooking. This was because we had no resources. The other issue of concern to her was the fact we had no safe drinking water on tap.

Through several trips to Chogoria, Diane worked hard to help us enjoy a smoke-free spacious kitchen with all the accessories like modern stove, fridge, juicer, shelves and utensils. She helped us enjoy the right to potable water by having a plumber fit tanks with filters and pipes to the new kitchen.

She organised an electrician to do the lighting, kitchen tilers, painters to paint the whole centre and a sewing lady to make new curtains, providing an income for these local people.

We finished the renovations in March 2019 and because of Diane's support, the Faraja Community Centre is an amazing place to enjoy delicious vegetables and fruits from our gardens and markets and make fresh juices.

We at Faraja and the whole community of Chogoria have benefitted from Diane's generosity. We know her as one of us who truly works towards empowering the people in a way that is respectful and friendly and does not intimidate.

The Faraja kitchen came to us as a miracle indeed. We had never imagined that we could have a modern kitchen. Not that we lacked vision. No, vision we had, but times were difficult financially. When the kitchen was built and equipped, it was like we were dreaming! Our dream had come true!

This kitchen took us from using charcoal to gas and electricity. This made our work at Faraja easier and enjoyable. I love this kitchen dearly because it has enabled me and the other ladies to cook for the children more efficiently.

As the children are growing up, I can provide age-appropriate information about health and support their goals for the future. At Faraja we can now offer counselling services over a cup of tea or coffee.

The kitchen gives us the opportunity to work with local women in preparing new types of meals. Some women have used these recipes to empower themselves to generate income.

The kitchen gives the youth a safe place to meet, have dialogue and socialise and avoid risky behaviours such as alcohol and substance abuse.

Lastly, the kitchen provides sustainability to the Faraja activities as it will eventually generate revenue to finance many exciting projects.

Looking back now, I realise it is rare that one meets a friend who has the true spirit of supporting another one to succeed in their lives. To me Diane has been that person who came over to turn my lack to plenty.

May the Lord bless her dearly.

Millicent Mukindia

Chapter 32

A Vision for the Future

Now in 2023, I'm 66 and it's been four years since I visited Chogoria in rural Kenya. I had planned to go every year to continue our positive work in the community.

What have I been doing all that time?

Like millions of people, my lifestyle and work and my goals and dreams were smashed in 2020, 2021 and 2022 due to governments enforcing lockdowns around the world. These bizarre lockdowns (usually a term used in prisons) crashed economies, destroyed jobs and businesses, disrupted education for children and youth, and damaged mental and physical health by isolating people in their homes and preventing freedom of movement and social contact, enforcing facemask wearing as a social norm and violating human rights.

These tyrannical actions of governments, on the pretence of a deadly virus, caused horrendous harm and trauma globally. The propaganda and scaremongering by governments and the mainstream media culminated in coercing five billion trusting people, including pregnant women, babies, children and teenagers, into having dangerous injections worldwide.

The terrible repercussions of the global 'scamdemic' are still being felt as sudden deaths, debilitating illnesses and vaccine injuries increase every day, although go mostly unreported, except for the deaths of celebrities and sporting stars. The truth has come out through films such as *Died Suddenly* on *Rumble* and *Safe and Effective, A Second Opinion*, available to watch on *Oracle Films.*

The UK Government *Yellow Car*d reported 1,641,357 adverse reactions to COVID-19 vaccines and 2459 deaths up to February 22, 2023. These figures represent a fraction of the injuries and deaths from the jabs because many casualties have not been officially recognised. And this is just the UK. Illnesses and deaths in the US, Canada, Australia, Europe, and other countries continue to mount up.

Millions of us, including reputable doctors, scientists, legal experts, journalists, rebels and regular people who could see through the sham, took to the city streets around the world. But our protest rallies were not reported. Some experts claim that these malevolent injections have been administered to reduce the global population over the coming years.

And dictatorial governments are attempting to roll out more control of our lives, through abolishing cash and imposing a central bank to monitor all financial transactions, constant surveillance by technology and restricting freedom of movement, turning our lives into a dystopian nightmare.

I spent those three years of craziness writing political articles and campaigning with *Stand In The Park* on Sunday mornings, passing out leaflets to inform people of the dangers of the toxic injections. I ran for Kent County Council as an Independent on a human rights platform, but voters sadly believed and trusted the ruling Conservative Party.

I was preventing from flying without being vaxed so could not travel to visit my elderly mum in Australia or return to Kenya to carry on our community projects. Thankfully, those restrictions have now been lifted.

Folkestone Frolics

When I returned from Kenya in 2019, I moved to the seaside town of Folkestone. My husband and I had separated in 2018, after 38 years together and later divorced. These days we are good friends with our friendship based on our strong family bond, as devoted parents, and grandparents. We are keepers of our memories, cherishing our shared history. We know each other deeply. And we are colleagues, publishing books together.

Our son and his wife have three gorgeous children and, in 2020, we were blessed with our fourth grandchild when our daughter and her husband had a beautiful baby boy. I travelled to London regularly to help and now he's an adorable super-active toddler.

In these past four years I have also looked after refugee lads from Africa, who had fled war and persecution to find safety in the UK (which, despite the hostile policies of the UK government, is their human right under the Declaration of Human Rights adopted by the United Nations in 1948 and the UK Human Rights Act of 2000.) These remarkable young men, who arrived as vulnerable teenagers, have succeeded in going to college and learning English and mastering trades and skills, with a heartfelt ambition to contribute to society.

We also spent a lot of time renovating my house and gardening while dancing and singing to Bob Marley. *Three Little Birds, One Love, Is This Love* and songs of hope filled the neighbourhood with happy vibes.

And I wrote inspiring magazine stories about extraordinary people who are making a difference. Because despite political oppression, the goodness of humanity prevails.

The Time Has Arrived

And now it is time to reclaim our dreams, revitalise our projects and rekindle friendships. I have missed my friends who suffered greatly through the cruel lockdowns with tourists, charity workers and medical experts for other countries banned from visiting Chogoria.

In subsistence communities, authorities telling people to 'stay home' in their humble dwellings condemned them to loneliness and hunger. There was no binge-watching Netflix for millions of people locked down in poor countries. And they were prohibited from selling their goods in the markets to earn a living.

But now, the hardships are behind us. The skies are blue, and the sun is shining in rural Kenya. The avocadoes, mangoes and bananas are ripe. The time has arrived. I plan to return to continue our work at the *Faraja Community Centre* in January 2024.

At the top of the To Do List are some practical projects including installing toilets and a septic tank, repairs and renovations to the building and creating a shady courtyard.

The goal is to prepare Faraja to become a training centre for facilitators of the Community Empowerment Program to go to remote villages throughout Kenya. The comprehensive training course aims to prevent Female Genital Cutting and child marriage and educate villagers about a wide range of health issues.

Millicent and I hope to partner with *Tostan* and the *Orchid Project* to make this possible.

I am also encouraging volunteers with building skills to come and pitch in. You will be warmly welcomed at the Snow Peak Hotel and will fall in love with the peaceful, kind community, just as I have. And there will be plenty of other projects for eager volunteers to help with.

Six Support Groups

Faraja will host get-togethers for six community groups: Children, (already in full swing) Youth, Mums and Babies, Women, Men and Elderly Folk. These groups can meet regularly to hear informative guest speakers, share problems, and socialise with conversation, music, games and healthy food and drinks. No more isolation. We humans are all social beings, and we need interaction and bonding with others to thrive.

Six Business Projects

Training Centre

The starring role of our centre will be training courses to prevent harmful practices and promote health knowledge for more than 40 ethnic groups and tribes living throughout the vast and spectacular country of Kenya, with a population of more than 55 million.

We hope to attract funding and partners to train facilitators in their own languages so they can return to teach everyone in their villages. This is a big dream. But the seed can start to grow in the heartland of Kenya and spread far and wide into all the remote regions. We aim to protect future generations, empowering them with knowledge to thrive.

Soap-making

My friend in Uganda, Joan Nalubega, is an amazing entrepreneur who runs an award-winning business called Uganics. Joan invented a malaria-prevention soap which is used in high-risk areas to protect adults and children from infection. Prevention is my favourite strategy to solve the problems blighting humanity. I have a dream to invite Joan to visit Faraja to teach local people how to make this natural soap to prevent malaria. Soap-making is another exciting business that our community centre can support.

Coconut Cheese

I love coconuts as much as I love avocados. Coconut Oil is a heroic Super Food. In the book, *The Coconut Oil Miracle*, author Bruce Fife, enthuses about the many health benefits, writing: "Coconut oil contains saturated fats found in mother's milk known as medium-chain fatty acids. People with a diet high in coconut oil are healthier with fewer incidences of heart disease, cancer, and digestive complaints."

And oil is just one element of the amazing coconut.

Coconuts provide hydrating coconut water, coconut oil, coconut milk and cream which can be made into cheese, desiccated coconut, coconut flour and coconut sugar and the shells can be stripped for garden mulch and polished to make bowls and the leaves of coconut trees can be woven into baskets. All this from the kooky coconut!

Garama and I hatched a business idea on my last trip to transport coconuts up from coastal Mombasa where they are grown in abundance, to make all of these healthy foods and useful products! Garama is highly skilled in the art of opening coconuts and extracting all the goodies in the traditional way having learned the skills growing up on a farm in Mombasa.

I'm especially excited about making cheese from coconut oil and milk because cheese is difficult to buy in the Chogoria and it's an essential ingredient in our delicious Faraja pizzas! Once we have yummy healthy coconut cheese there will be no stopping our enthusiastic pizza makers!

Sewing

Faraja will support small businesses including the Sewing Project making aprons, bags and clothing and other items to sell. Many Chogorian ladies are talented sewers and many of my friends in Australia and the UK are skilled craftswomen who would enjoy creating colourful African products to generate income for local families.

The Faraja Café

While local people have plenty of home-grown healthy veggies, fruits and grains to make traditional dishes such as Ugali, Mukimo and Githeri, we want to introduce the locals to fresh fruit juices, bean burgers, pasta, Mexican dishes, muffins and biscuits and of course irresistible pizza!

With a steady flow of tourists enroute to hike Mount Kenya and a variety of international workers at the hospital, local charities and churches, we believe Faraja Café could be a successful business, generating funds to cover the running costs of the kitchen and support outreach projects.

Volunteers with a passion for cooking will be warmly welcomed. As the locals say in Swahali, *Karibu.*

Support for Local Businesses

And finally, Faraja aims to support local farmers, such as the respected elder and legendary coffee grower, Mr Justin Njeru, to turn their abundant produce into saleable products.

The tropical region is rich in healthy foods. It is time for local people to be enriched by their labours. Time for hard-working farmers to prosper.

Time for Kenya, and the whole of Africa, to flourish.

Can all these ambitious projects be achieved through one little community centre in the middle of Kenya?

'From Little Things Big Things Grow' is an optimistic song by Kev Carmody and Paul Kelly, champions of the indigenous First Nations people of Australia who migrated from Africa 50,000 year ago.

African people are intelligent, caring, strong and resilient. For them, if given the opportunities, anything is possible.

Chapter 33

My Favourite Charities

If you have a heart to help, consider supporting these outstanding charities.

Faraja Community Centre is a registered charity with the Social Services in Kenya. Founded by Millicent Mukindia in 2003, the centre in Chogoria, in Tharaka-Nitha county, is dedicated to helping vulnerable children and providing health education to people living in remote areas.

https://www.farajacenterkenya.org/

Tostan is a non-profit organisation based in Senegal, founded by Molly Melching in 1991. The highly successful organisation works to prevent female genital cutting (FGC) and child marriage throughout West Africa, through grassroots health and human rights education in villages.

https://tostan.org

The Orchid Project is a UK-based charity supporting the global movement to end FGC, partnering with organisations around the world, including Tostan. Founded by Julia Lalla-Maharajh OBE in 2010, the Orchid Project is powered by a dedicated team and loyal funding supporters.

https://www.orchidproject.org/

Hamlin Fistula UK was founded by Australian Obstetrician and Gynaecologist, Dr Catherine Hamlin AC and her husband Dr Reginald Hamlin OBE in Addis Ababa, Ethiopia. The dedicated doctors performed reconstructive surgery on women suffering with obstetric fistulas, injuries caused in childbirth.

Six Hamlin Fistula Hospitals across Ethiopia have treated more than 60,000 women over the past 60 years. After Reginald died in 1993, Catherine carried on running the hospitals until she died at the age of 96 in 2020. Their great work continues.

https://hamlinfistulauk.org/

Sightsavers works in more than 30 countries to restore the eyesight of children and adults suffering from blindness, prevent avoidable blindness and fight for the rights of people with disabilities. This extraordinary organisation was founded by British couple, Sir John Wilson, who was blind, and his wife Lady Jean Wilson in 1950.

Blindness is my worst fear. I donate to this charity every month.

https://www.sightsavers.org

Charity: Water was founded by New York Nightclub Promoter, Scott Harrison in 2006, who was shocked to discover that 771 million people lack basic access to clean and safe drinking water. The dynamic charity has funded over 120,000 water projects helping more than 16 million people in 29 countries.

I cannot accept that people do not have their basis survival need of clean water. I donate to this charity every month.

https://www.charitywater.org/uk/

Because International supplies *Shoes That Grow* to school children in poor communities, protecting them from soil-transmitted diseases, including parasites called jiggers.

The charity wad founded by Kenton Lee, a college graduate from Idaho, America.

His inspiring success story shows the power of a light bulb moment! In 2007, Kenton volunteered in an orphanage in Nairobi. When he noticed a little girl wearing shoes that were so small her toes were sticking out, he thought: 'What if there was a shoe that could adjust and expand its size?'

It took Kenton and his friends six years to perfect the design of the innovative shoes. Shoes That Grow are now manufactured in Mombasa, Kenya, creating jobs for locals, and 380,000 pairs have been distributed to kids and families worldwide.

https://becauseinternational.org/

Uganics is a social enterprise founded by entrepreneur, Joan Nalubega. Growing up in an orphanage in Uganda, Joan suffers many bouts of malaria, causing her to miss school. After studying at the Social Innovative Academy, she developed an organic mosquito-repellent soap to protect families in vulnerable communities.

Through using the soap daily, mothers can protect themselves and their children against one of the biggest killers in Uganda. There are 10,000 malaria deaths a year in Uganda and one million people die every year globally from the preventable disease. Joan also manufactures and sells beautiful essential oil products that fund the distribution of malaria-prevention soap.

https://www.uganics.org/

The Halimah Trust in Pakistan was founded by the remarkable Dr Zareen Roohi Ahmed. After her beautiful daughter was murdered, Zareen channelled her heart-breaking grief into building a school for 1600 orphaned girls in Pakistan. She created the life-changing charity in her daughter's name.

https://www.halimahtrust.org.uk/

Zareen, who grew up in the West Midlands of England, went on to create the social enterprise, **Gift Wellness**, helping girls and women in refugee camps by supplying eco-friendly, non-toxic sanitary products.

In 10 years, she has distributed over six million period products globally. She also manufactures an exquisite range of essential oil soaps.

I had the pleasure of interviewing Zareen and writing her inspiring story for the UK magazine My Weekly.

https://giftwellness.co.uk/

Dr Karambu Ringera runs the **Tiriji Foundation**, the *Amani Home for Children* orphaned through HIV/AIDS, and *International Peace Initiatives.*

The joyful children's home and tranquil retreat are based in Meru, Kenya, amidst lush food forests and flourishing permaculture gardens, where the former University lecturer runs empowering courses for youth including the New Generation Leaders Program and regeneration and sustainable agriculture.

I was honoured to visit Karambu and awe-struck by the idyllic oasis of love and hope she's created.

https://tirijifoundation.com/

Medic Outpost is dedicated to training and equipping first responders in rural areas ravaged by conflict, famine, and inadequate infrastructure. Founder Larry Hill, a rugged Texan, has devoted three decades to field medical care for indigenous communities and refugees in remote locations worldwide.

Medic Outpost has treated more than 10,000 children in the slums of Nairobi for intestinal parasites and vitamin deficiencies. The children are also educated in hygiene and first aid, saving countless lives.

I became friends with Larry in Chogoria in 2018, when he told me about his dream to start a medical service for neglected communities in Kenya. I have witnessed his charity grow from a challenging idea into an unstoppable force for good.

https://www.medicoutpost.org/

Three formidable Wildlife Warriors, Angela Sheldrick, Saba Douglas-Hamilton and Kuki Gallmann have devoted their lives to protecting elephants, endangered species and precious wilderness in Kenya.

The Sheldrick Wildlife Trust runs the famous Elephant Orphanage in Nairobi led by CEO Angela Sheldrick. The charity rescues and raises baby elephants orphaned by abhorrent poaching and harsh droughts. After years of intensive devotion by keepers, adolescent elephants are returned to the wild, where they play a vital role in the ecology.

Founded by Dame Daphne Sheldrick, the family charity has been dedicated to protecting wildlife and habitat in Kenya for 45 years. Tourists come from all over the world to see the adorable baby elephants and support this worthy cause.

I had the honour of interviewing Angela and writing her story for the UK magazine, My Weekly. Angela kindly invited me to go behind the scenes and meet their smallest baby, little Pili, who was just three weeks old when rescued clinging to a pepper tree after his mother died in the drought. Meeting sweet little Pili up close was such a touching experience. I made a little video about the encounter on YouTube.

https://www.sheldrickwildlifetrust.org/

Save the Elephants was started by acclaimed zoologist, Iain Douglas-Hamilton in 1993 and is now led by his extraordinary daughter, Saba Douglas-Hamilton in Samburu National Park in the Great Rift Valley in Kenya.

Saba is well-known through the enthralling BBC TV series, *This Wild Life* that documents the challenges of managing the family's tourist resort and their dramatic field work rescuing elephants in danger.

I was delighted to hear Saba give an eloquent and heartfelt talk about the plight of elephants and their inspiring conservation work, at the Leas Cliff Hall in Folkestone in 2022.

https://www.savetheelephants.org/

Kuki Gallmann has devoted her life to protecting the wildlife and unique wilderness of Laikipia, west of Mount Kenya, since migrating from Italy in 1972.

A fierce environmental activist, she became passionate about protecting her new homeland since her husband, Paola and son, Emanuele both died young in tragic accidents, and left Kuki and her daughter, Sveve to carry on their legacy. **The Gallmann Memorial Foundation** cares for a spectacular 98,000 acre Conservancy in Ol Ari Nyiro.

When I read Kuki's autobiography, I Dreamed Of Africa I was captivated by her inspiring story of overcoming grief to become a mighty champion for the spectacular, untamed environment of Laikipia, providing habitat for countless species of endangered animals.

https://gallmannkenya.org/

I love all these charities because they were started by passionate individuals with a grand vision. By following their hearts, these ordinary people turned into extraordinary heroes. They discovered practical, effective solutions to overcome challenging problems, making a profound difference to humanity, animals, and the planet.

About the Author

Diane Priestley is an experienced Journalist with a diverse career spanning more than 40 years writing for newspapers, magazines and online publications in Australia and the UK.

She is also a qualified Counsellor, trained in developmental psychology, personality types, inner child therapy, relationships, communication skills and community development.

An Aussie living in the UK since 2009, Diane is involved with community work in Kenya in partnership with dedicated local people, volunteers, and charities.

Her passion for Making a Difference in Africa was sparked in her 50s and now her idealistic vision is becoming a reality.

Contact Diane at *dianejoypriestley@gmail.com*

Printed in Great Britain
by Amazon

23495973R00118